# PLANTS
### AND
## PLANT LIFE

## VOLUME 4
## Plant Ecology

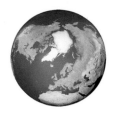

# MICHAEL ALLABY

GROLIER
EDUCATIONAL

# About this Set

**PLANTS AND PLANT LIFE** *is a ten-volume set that describes the world of plants in all its facets. Volume by volume, you will be introduced to the many different aspects of plant life.*

*The first three volumes (1: Roots, Stems, and Leaves, 2: Flowers and Fruits, and 3: Life Processes) explain the basic structure, reproductive methods, and processes of life in flowering plants.*

*Volume 4 (Plant Ecology) explores the place of plants in the living community of life on Earth, while Volume 5 (Plants Used by People) presents the literally hundreds of plants that have been exploited by people for food, clothing, building, and many other uses.*

*The final five volumes (6: Algae and Fungi, 7: Mosses and Ferns, 8: Conifers, 9: Flowering Plants—The Monocotyledons, and 10: Flowering Plants—The Dicotyledons) lead the reader on a journey of discovery through the main groups of life that are usually classed as plants. In these volumes the typical and characteristic features of each group and its components are clearly outlined.*

*Though each volume deals with a distinct aspect of plant life, many of them are interrelated. To help you understand these links, every entry has enlightening cross-references to other entries and volumes. Throughout the set you will also find special short boxed features— entitled "Protecting Our World"—that focus on particular stories of environmental concern.*

*The whole set is liberally illustrated with diagrams explaining plant processes and structures, with depictions of typical plants and maps showing global distribution. In addition, hundreds of photographs bring the world of plants vividly to life. At the end of every volume there is a useful glossary explaining the technical terms that are used in the text, an index to all the volumes in the set, and finally, a list of other sources of reference (both books and websites). All the plants mentioned in the volume are listed alphabetically by common name, with their scientific names alongside.*

# Contents

Published 2001 by Grolier Educational, Danbury, CT 06816

This edition published exclusively for the school and library market

Planned and produced by Andromeda Oxford Limited, 11–13 The Vineyard, Abingdon, Oxon OX14 3PX, UK
www.andromeda.co.uk

Copyright © Andromeda Oxford Limited 2001

**Project Director:** *Graham Bateman*
**Editorial Manager:** *Peter Lewis*
**Art Editors and Designers:** *Martin Anderson, Chris Munday, Steve McCurdy*
**Editors:** *Penelope Isaac, Eleanor Stillwell*
**Cartography:** *Richard Watts, Tim Williams*
**Editorial Assistant:** *Marian Dreier*
**Picture Manager:** *Claire Turner*
**Production:** *Clive Sparling*
**Index:** *Ann Barrett*

Originated and printed in Hong Kong

**Library of Congress Cataloging-in-Publication Data**

Plants and plant life.
        p.      cm.
   Includes bibliographical references.
   Contents: v.1. Roots, stems, and leaves -- v. 2. Flowers and fruits -- v. 3. Life processes -- v. 4. Plant ecology -- v. 5. Plants used by people -- v. 6. Algae and fungi -- v. 7. Mosses and ferns -- v. 8. Conifers -- v. 9. Flowering plants--the Monocotyledons -- v. 10. Flowering plants--the Dicotyledons.
   ISBN 0-7172-9510-9 (set : alk. paper) -- ISBN 0-7172-9514-1 (vol. 4)
     1. Plants--Juvenile literature. 2. Botany--Juvenile literature. [1.Plants--Encyclopedias. 2. Botany--Encyclopedias.] 1. Grolier Educational Corporation.

QK49 .P54 2000
580--dc21
                                99-056140

Set ISBN  0–7172–9510–9

Volume 4 ISBN  0–7172–9514–1

# Plants and the Ecosystem

PLANTS ARE EVERYWHERE. WE SEE THEM ALL AROUND US, in gardens and parks, on empty plots, and even pushing up through cracks in the sidewalk. Out of town there are even more plants, of course. Farmers and gardeners have planted some, but the plants we see growing naturally are of many kinds.

Usually different types of plants grow side by side, all mixed up. A field may look as though there is only grass growing in it; but if you look closely, you will see there are different kinds of grass, and there are other small plants growing among them. Walk into a forest, and you will see several different kinds of tree and many other plants growing on the ground between the trees.

All of these plants affect each other. Trees shade the ground, for example, making conditions difficult for small plants that need plenty of sunshine. They may take a large amount of water from the ground, leaving the soil around their roots too dry for some plants, but suitable for those that cannot grow in wet ground.

Animals eat plants, and they have preferences, just as we do. Some animals prefer the leaves of one plant, others eat the roots of another; some eat seeds, some fruit, and some even eat wood. Carnivorous (meat-eating) animals feed on the herbivores (plant-eaters), and they seek out the particular food that suits them. Different animals live among different groups of plants.

## The Study of Households

The plants and animals living together in a particular place are like the members of a household. Each has its own needs and its own contribution to make. The Greek word for house is *oikos*; *logos* means "explanation." In 1866 the German zoologist Ernst Haeckel (1834–1919) combined the two words to coin the term *ökologie*. In English we know it as ecology.

Ecology is the branch of science that aims to explain how plant and animal households work. Ecologists study the relationships among the members of these households and the ways changes in the fortunes of one member affect the others.

## Ecosystems

Plants use sunlight as a source of energy to drive chemical reactions that produce sugars from carbon dioxide and water. The process is

▶ Aspens showing their magnificent fall colors in the Sierra Nevada Mountains, California.

called photosynthesis. They also take substances from the soil and use them to build their own tissues. Animals eat the tissues and discard the parts they cannot digest in their bodily wastes. This provides food for other organisms. Eventually, the substances taken from the soil are returned to it and absorbed again by plant roots.

Energy from the Sun in the form of sugars and minerals from the ground is constantly passing from one group of living organisms to another. When this activity is studied as a whole, together with the relationships among the organisms performing it, it becomes clear that the living organisms, together with all the physical and chemical components of their surroundings, make up a system, in which changes in one place produce changes in another. Ecologists describe this as an "ecological system," which is shortened to "ecosystem."

## Ecosystems Large and Small

An ecosystem can be large or small. A puddle of water can be an ecosystem, and a vast forest is also an ecosystem. The plants typical of an entire region of the Earth, such as tropical forest, desert, or grassland, are known as a "biome." A biome contains many local ecosystems.

Within an ecosystem there are places where the physical and chemical conditions suit particular species. Among the scattered trees of an area of woodland, for example, enough sunshine reaches the ground to allow grasses to thrive. Deer graze there and feel safe from their enemies, because if danger threatens, they can quickly hide among the trees. The open glades and clearings among the trees are where the deer live. They make up what is known as the habitat of the deer.

The habitat of a plant or animal is where it lives. It is the type of surroundings that suit it and where you might expect to find it. Woodland glades and clearings can be described as "deer habitat," for example; the description is correct even if no deer are living there because if the habitat is suitable, any deer finding their way into it would thrive.

For the time that the plant or animal lives there the habitat, together with the food, water, shelter, and other resources it

## A WOODLAND

A woodland in a European river valley is an ecosystem that contains many habitats. The  trees are widely spaced; between them grasses and herbs provide pasture for large grazing animals, such as fallow deer (*Dama dama*) and wisent, or European bison (*Bison bonasus*). This is their habitat. Rabbits (*Oryctolagus cuniculus*) graze the short grass. Their habitat includes soft earth in which they can dig their burrows. The trees provide sites for birds to nest and are also the habitat for gray squirrels (*Sciurus carolinensis*) and many insects. Fungi grow on decaying wood. Fish and frogs are hunted by the kingfisher (*Alcedo atthis*). Water voles (*Arvicola terrestris*) live in the river bank, and hedge-hogs (*Erinaceus europaeus*) hunt invertebrates in the soft ground.

provides, are known as its niche. Suppose a seed falls to the ground, and a young plant begins to grow. It will survive only if it has landed on open ground where no bigger plant shades it. It needs nourishment, which its roots will find only if other plants have not already removed it from the soil. It needs water, so it will grow only if there is moisture within reach of its roots. Until the plant arrived, the space, sunlight, soil minerals, and water were not being used. As soon as the young plant starts to use them, it is said to be occupying a niche. In other words, the organism defines the niche by exploiting resources that remained unused until it arrived.

Once members of a particular species arrive, establish themselves, and make full use of the resources, no other species can gain access to the resources without displacing the first species. If members of two species try to use the same resources in exactly the same way, eventually one of the species will prevail, and the other will disappear. This is called competitive exclusion.

## Biomes, Ecosystems, Communities, Populations

Ecological terms have quite precise meanings. In addition to "biome," "ecosystem," "habitat," and "niche," there are two more: "community" and "population." A biome is named after the dominant type of vegetation found in a particular region of the world and contains many ecosystems. Each ecosystem is made up of habitats, which are the physical, chemical, and biological conditions in which plants and animals can live, together with the communities that live in them.

Communities consist of populations of particular species. All the members of a particular species living in the same ecosystem are called a population. For example, many American forests contain aspen trees, so those ecosystems have populations of aspens. All the forest trees together make up a community.

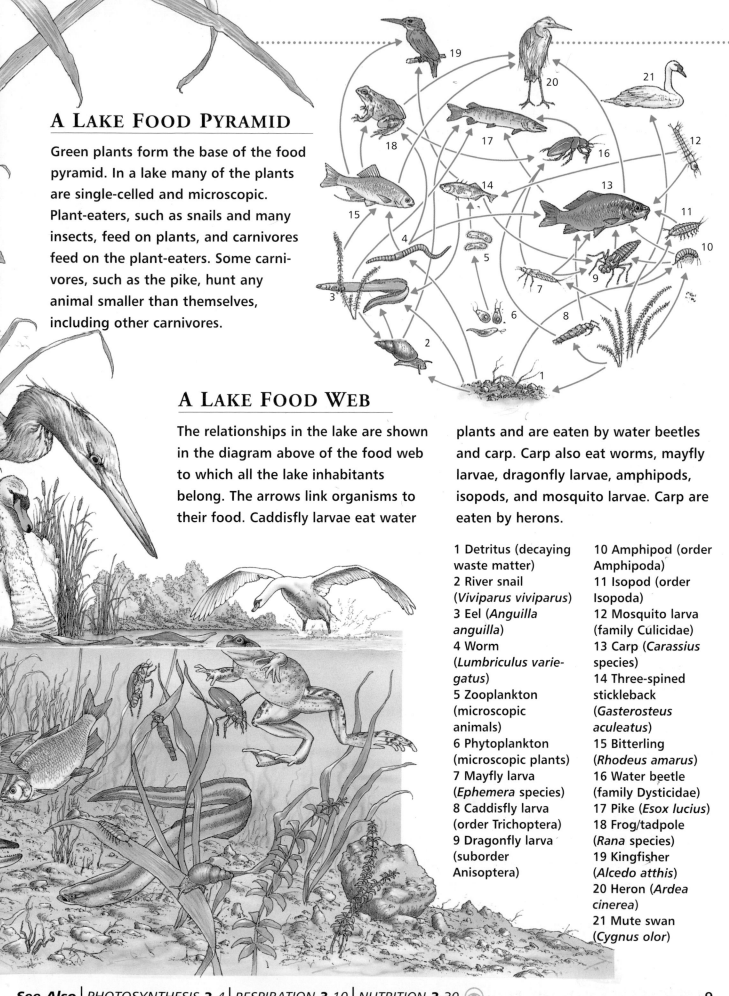

## A LAKE FOOD PYRAMID

Green plants form the base of the food pyramid. In a lake many of the plants are single-celled and microscopic. Plant-eaters, such as snails and many insects, feed on plants, and carnivores feed on the plant-eaters. Some carnivores, such as the pike, hunt any animal smaller than themselves, including other carnivores.

## A LAKE FOOD WEB

The relationships in the lake are shown in the diagram above of the food web to which all the lake inhabitants belong. The arrows link organisms to their food. Caddisfly larvae eat water plants and are eaten by water beetles and carp. Carp also eat worms, mayfly larvae, dragonfly larvae, amphipods, isopods, and mosquito larvae. Carp are eaten by herons.

1 Detritus (decaying waste matter)
2 River snail (*Viviparus viviparus*)
3 Eel (*Anguilla anguilla*)
4 Worm (*Lumbriculus variegatus*)
5 Zooplankton (microscopic animals)
6 Phytoplankton (microscopic plants)
7 Mayfly larva (*Ephemera* species)
8 Caddisfly larva (order Trichoptera)
9 Dragonfly larva (suborder Anisoptera)

10 Amphipod (order Amphipoda)
11 Isopod (order Isopoda)
12 Mosquito larva (family Culicidae)
13 Carp (*Carassius* species)
14 Three-spined stickleback (*Gasterosteus aculeatus*)
15 Bitterling (*Rhodeus amarus*)
16 Water beetle (family Dysticidae)
17 Pike (*Esox lucius*)
18 Frog/tadpole (*Rana* species)
19 Kingfisher (*Alcedo atthis*)
20 Heron (*Ardea cinerea*)
21 Mute swan (*Cygnus olor*)

## Food Chains and Food Webs

Food is the most important of the resources that organisms need; many of the relationships within an ecosystem are based on feeding behavior. An insect might be eating the leaf of a tree when an insect-eating bird snatches it. As the bird flies away, a bird-eating hawk seizes it. This sequence of events can be summarized as leaf→insect→bird 1→bird 2. This is called a food chain because it places the organisms in a line.

In the real world it is rarely so simple because there are very few animals that eat only one kind of food. Frogs eat flying insects, which they catch with their long, sticky tongues, but they also eat parts of plants and small insects and insect larvae that they take from water. Most insect-eating birds also eat seeds in the fall, when seeds are abundant but there are fewer insects around. This more realistic picture of relationships can be shown as a food web, though most food-web diagrams are still very simplified.

## Pyramids, and Why Nothing Hunts Owls

If plants vanish, there will be nothing for herbivores to eat, and all animals will starve. On the other hand, if plants are plentiful, there will be more for herbivores. They will be healthier, produce more offspring, and will provide more food for carnivores. From a feeding point of view the plants, herbivores, and carnivores seem to occupy distinct levels: plants are at the bottom, herbivores next, then carnivores, and finally carnivore-eating carnivores.

A diagram showing the relationships takes the form of a stepped pyramid. Each population is represented by a rectangle. The plants, at the base, form the biggest rectangle. The herbivores form a smaller one, the carnivores a still smaller one, and the top carnivores the smallest rectangle of all. This is known as an ecological pyramid. The plants are called producers because they are the only organisms that manufacture food (by photosynthesis). All animals are consumers. The herbivores are primary consumers; carnivores at the first level are secondary consumers. Above them are tertiary consumers.

The food that passes from each level to the next also represents energy. Our bodies need energy to allow us to move, think, digest food, and to maintain a constant internal temperature. We obtain this energy from the food we eat, and that food comes directly or indirectly from plants, the producers. They

sunlight energy

plants

herbivores

energy flow

heat loss

## RECYCLING ENERGY

Energy moves from one group to another in an ecosystem. Sunlight supplies green plants with the energy for photosynthesis. Here, rabbits obtain energy by eating plants, and a barn owl by eating rabbits. Waste products and remains of dead plants and animals provide food for decomposers.

decomposers

carnivores

obtained it from sunlight. So our food is made with the energy of sunlight, and we use most of it in our own bodies.

Other animals are no different: they use about 90 percent of their food energy. This leaves 10 percent available for the animal that eats them, so it takes a large number of plants to feed one

rabbit and many rabbits to feed one owl. Owls need so much space to find enough food for themselves that they are widely dispersed. No animal hunts them because it would use more energy in the hunt than it could obtain from the quarry.

# The Water Cycle

ALL THE WATER WE USE WAS ONCE PART OF THE OCEAN. When we pour it away, it begins a journey that eventually takes it back to the ocean. It is constantly on the move between sea, air, and land. This movement forms a cycle that begins and ends in the sea. It is called the water, or hydrological, cycle.

Oceans and seas cover over 70 percent of the surface of the Earth and contain 97 percent of all the water on Earth. They are made up of salt water, though, which is poisonous to most land-dwelling plants and animals. However, when salt water evaporates or freezes, the salt is removed. It is then fresh water that plants can absorb and use, and animals are able to drink.

## Water, Water, Everywhere

More than half of all the fresh water on Earth exists as ice and snow in glaciers, and in the ice sheets of Greenland, the Arctic, and Antarctica. There is also fresh water below ground, but about 0.5 percent of it is so far below the surface that it is unavailable. The remainder is less than 1 percent of all the water on the planet, which amounts to about 4 billion billion gallons (15 billion billion liters). It has to satisfy all the needs of every land-dwelling plant and animal.

Water evaporates from the sea, lakes, rivers, and wet ground.

Plants release it through transpiration. Evaporation changes liquid water into water vapor, a gas. Each year about 89 million billion gallons (337 million billion liters) evaporate from the oceans and about 17 million billion gallons (64 million billion liters) from the land and plants.

Water vapor condenses to form clouds of liquid droplets, which fall as rain, hail, or snow. About 79 million billion gallons (300 million billion liters) fall over the oceans and 26 million billion gallons (98 million billion liters) over land. Some of the water falling on the land evaporates again, but about 9.5 million billion gallons (36 million billion liters) drain into rivers flowing back to the sea. A molecule of water spends an average of 4,000 years in the ocean, 400 years on land, and 10 days in the air.

## Plants, Water, and Transpiration

Plants must capture water that falls as rain or snow before it escapes. Their roots absorb it, together with nutrients dissolved into it, from the soil. Once inside a plant, the water is transported to every part of it. As well as conveying nutrients, the water helps keep cells rigid (turgid). This gives the plant physical support.

There are small pores (stomata) in the leaves and stems of every plant: they open to allow gas exchange. This is vital to the plant; but when the pores are open, water can evaporate through them. This is the process of transpiration. To replace the water lost in this way, the plant must absorb more from the ground, so there is a steady flow of water from the ground, into the roots, through the plant, and into the air.

## Ground Water, Aquifers, and the Water Table

Water not absorbed by plants either runs off the surface and into rivers or soaks into the soil. Eventually it reaches a layer of rock or clay that it cannot penetrate. The water accumulates above this surface, but at the same time, it flows over the surface of the rock or clay, moving downhill.

This water, known as ground water, flows slowly between soil particles. The material through which it moves is an aquifer. The ground water saturates the aquifer; the upper edge of the saturated layer is called the water table. If rain falls faster than ground water can flow away, the water table will rise. If rain persists, the water table may reach the surface. The soil is then waterlogged. Plants will die because their roots cannot exchange gases.

▶ Plants draw water from the ground and release it into the air. It may then condense to form mist and clouds. This is highland cloud forest in Malaysia.

## THE WATER CYCLE

This diagram shows the part of the water cycle that affects the land. Water falls as rain or snow. Some evaporates from rivers, lakes, and wet ground. Some passes through plants and is released by transpiration. A very small amount is returned by plant and animal respiration.

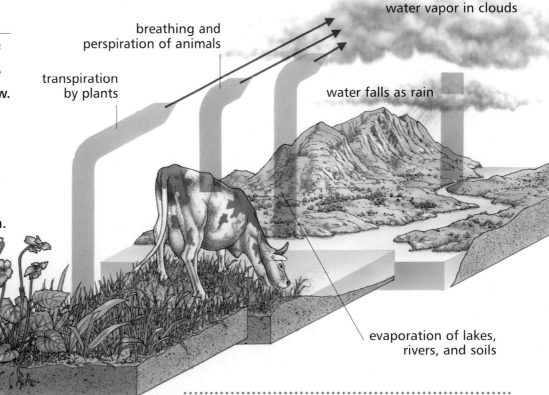

water vapor in clouds

breathing and perspiration of animals

transpiration by plants

water falls as rain

evaporation of lakes, rivers, and soils

**See Also** | ROOTS **1** 22 | WATER & WATER UPTAKE **3** 24 | PREHISTORIC PLANTS **7** 18 👁

# The Carbon Cycle

EVERY LIVING CELL CONTAINS CARBON, and air-breathing plants and animals also use it to provide energy. We obtain the carbon our bodies need from our food; it comes directly, or indirectly, from green plants. They obtain their carbon from the air, using photosynthesis to make sugars from carbon dioxide gas and water.

Every year a very small amount of carbon dioxide is released into the air by erupting volcanoes, and a small amount is permanently removed by being buried on the seabed. This happens when some marine organisms, living inside shells they have made from calcium carbonate (using carbon compounds dissolved in the seawater around them), die. Their shells sink to the seafloor, and eventually they may become chalk or limestone rock.

Carbon is also stored in the form of coal, gas, and oil. They are called fossil fuels because they are made from the remains of plants and animals that lived many millions of years ago.

## Carbon for Plants and Animals

Plants obtain their carbon from carbon dioxide gas, which is present as about 0.03 percent by volume of the air around us.

Some carbon dioxide dissolves in river water and is carried toward the sea. As it travels, the carbon dioxide takes part in chemical reactions that convert it into bicarbonate and carbonate. They are the forms in which marine organisms use the carbon to make their shells.

Using sunlight energy, green plants make sugars from carbon dioxide and water. The plants use the sugars in their own cells, but animals can obtain them by eating the plants. So carbon passes from the air to plants and from plants to animals.

Waste products from plants and animals—and their dead tissues—also contain carbon. In this form the carbon is available to fungi, bacteria, and other organisms. They are called decomposers because they break down plant and animal materials into simple chemical compounds.

## Returning Carbon to the Air

Energy is released when carbon combines with oxygen to make carbon dioxide. All air-breathing organisms obtain energy in this way through respiration. Once the energy has been released, the cells have no further use for the carbon dioxide. It is expelled into the air. Plants both absorb carbon dioxide and emit it.

---

**PROTECTING OUR WORLD**

## FIRE

When vegetation burns, its carbon is returned to the air as carbon dioxide. This does not increase the amount of carbon dioxide in the air because the amount returned to the air is exactly the same as the amount that was removed by photosynthesis to make the plants.

Burning coal, oil, and gas is different. It returns to the air carbon that was stored millions of years ago, and it may disturb the balance of the carbon cycle. Many scientists fear that adding to the amount of carbon in the air will alter the climate and increase temperatures.

# THE CARBON CYCLE

**Carbon is present in the air as carbon dioxide ($CO_2$). It passes from the air to plants and animals, and then returns to the air. Burning fossil fuels releases carbon stored millions of years ago. Volcanoes also release carbon dioxide.**

As they break down dead and discarded plant and animal material, the decomposers also convert carbon into carbon dioxide. Eventually, all the carbon contained in living cells is oxidized in this way. The carbon that is removed from the air by photosynthesis is returned to the air by respiration. This completes the cycle. The amounts that are returned to the air balance the amounts that are removed from it.

▼ **Controlled burning of vegetation in California in preparation for planting more trees.**

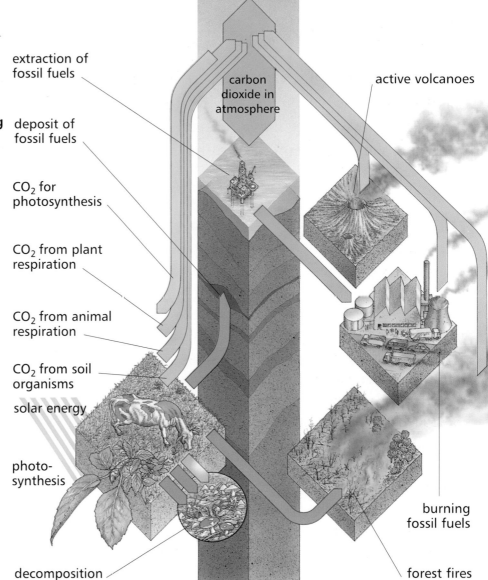

extraction of fossil fuels

carbon dioxide in atmosphere

active volcanoes

deposit of fossil fuels

$CO_2$ for photosynthesis

$CO_2$ from plant respiration

$CO_2$ from animal respiration

$CO_2$ from soil organisms

solar energy

photosynthesis

decomposition

burning fossil fuels

forest fires

# The Nitrogen Cycle

ALL PROTEINS CONTAIN NITROGEN. It is in every living cell, and without it life would be impossible. Air is 78 percent nitrogen by volume; but although we breathe it constantly, we exhale it again unaltered. We cannot make use of nitrogen gas, and neither can any other animal. Animals obtain their nitrogen from the plants they eat.

Plants also cannot absorb nitrogen gas and need help to obtain nitrogen. Some of that help is provided by lightning, but most comes from microscopic, single-celled organisms.

Nitrogen gas does not react readily with other substances. That is why plants cannot incorporate it directly: it will not form compounds with any of the contents of their tissues.

Lightning releases enough energy to force nitrogen to react with oxygen. The oxidized nitrogen dissolves in cloud droplets, where it forms nitric acid that is washed to the ground by rain. This is nitrogen in a form plants can use, but it accounts for no more than 4 percent of the nitrogen absorbed by plants.

## THE NITROGEN CYCLE

Nitrogen enters the air from volcanic eruptions. It is converted into soluble compounds by bacteria, lightning, and in factories that make fertilizer. It is used by plants and animals to build proteins and is returned to the air by bacteria.

### Nitrogen Fixation

Most nitrogen is made to react by microorganisms present in the soil. The organisms make nitrogen react with hydrogen to form ammonia. This reaction is called nitrogen "fixation." Nitrogen-fixing bacteria, which belong to the genus *Rhizobium,* infect the roots of certain plants, especially legumes. It is a large family (Fabaceae) that includes beans,

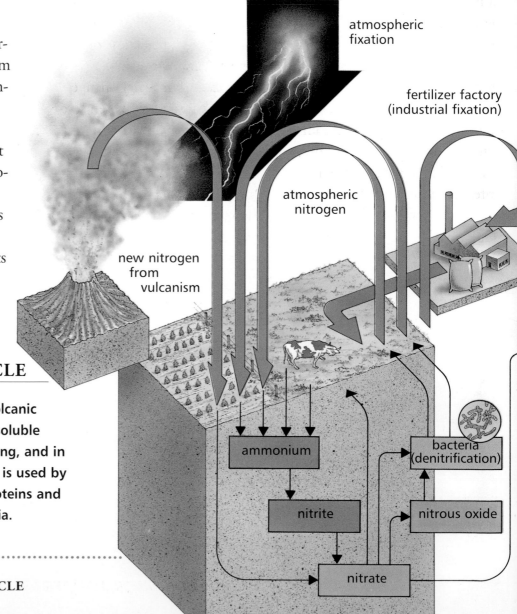

atmospheric fixation

fertilizer factory (industrial fixation)

atmospheric nitrogen

new nitrogen from vulcanism

ammonium

nitrite

nitrate

bacteria (denitrification)

nitrous oxide

▶ Rice plants in this paddy in Luzon, Philippines, are nourished with nitrogen provided by cyanobacteria in the water.

peas, alfalfa, and lupins. The *Rhizobium* bacteria form visible colonies, called nodules, on the outside of the roots.

Other nitrogen-fixing bacteria, including species of the genera *Azotobacter* and *Clostridium,* also live in the soil, but do not attach themselves to plant roots. Water often contains bacteria, called cyanobacteria, that make sugars by photosynthesis. Some, such as the genus *Anabaena,* fix nitrogen.

Nitric acid, from rain, changes to nitrate in the soil, where plants are able to absorb it. Some plants can also absorb ammonia from soil organisms, but most of it is converted to nitrate before it enters plant roots.

The process called nitrification is carried out by other groups of bacteria, including those of the genera *Nitrosomonas* and *Nitrobacter.* First, they change ammonia into nitrite, then into nitrate. Nitrate and ammonia are both soluble in water, and plant roots absorb them in liquid form. Not all the nitrogen is absorbed. Some drains into waterways to be used by water plants.

In plants amino acids—the chemical units from which proteins are built—contain the element nitrogen. Animals that eat the plants obtain the amino acids, from which their bodies construct the proteins they need.

## Recycling Nitrogen

Plant and animal wastes, and the remains of dead organisms, still contain proteins. Organisms that eat this material break its chemical content into simple compounds. Bacteria then convert the amino acids into ammonia or compounds of ammonium. This returns the nitrogen to the bacteria that carry out nitrification.

Not all of the nitrogen is recycled, however. Some bacteria get the oxygen they need from nitrate and release nitrogen gas as a waste product. This process is called denitrification, and it completes the nitrogen cycle.

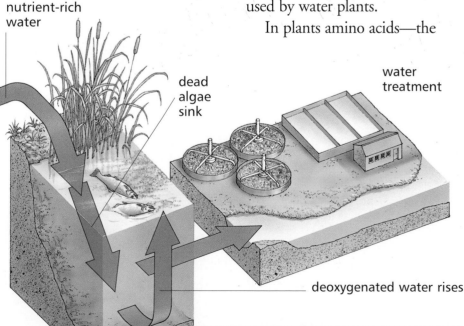

nutrient-rich water

dead algae sink

water treatment

deoxygenated water rises

*See Also* | NITROGEN FIXATION **3** *34* | BEAN FAMILY **10** *30* ◉

# Soil

SOIL IS HOME TO A VERY COMPLEX LIVING COMMUNITY. Plants obtain mineral nutrients and water from it. Soil also anchors them, so they are not blown or washed away. Plant and animal wastes are broken down for recycling in the soil by the very efficient animals, fungi, and bacteria that live in it.

Rub a little soil between your fingers. Just how gritty it feels depends on the size of the particles from which it is made. If they are large, like sand grains, the soil will feel very rough. If they are tiny, like silt, the soil will feel silky-smooth. If they are minute, like clay, the soil will stick together so well that you can roll it into a long "sausage" without it breaking. Soils are classified as sandy, loam, silty, or clays according to the proportions of sand, silt, and clay particles in them.

Although soil contains a huge community of living organisms, it consists mainly of mineral particles that were once bound together in solid rock.

## Weathering

Little by little, over very many years, rock is shattered and crumbles. The Sun heats its surface, making the outside of the rock expand more than the inside. This splits the rock; and when it next rains heavily, small fragments wash from it.

Alternate heating and cooling creates tiny cracks. Water seeps into them, and in winter it freezes. Water expands when it freezes, so this widens and deepens the cracks. Eventually, large blocks shatter. Each time a large rock breaks into several smaller ones, the total surface area increases, so more rock is exposed to the elements. The process is called weathering.

Boulders and smaller rocks roll down hills, bash into each other, and bounce on the solid rock beneath them. This produces more fragments. Small pieces are blown by the wind and smashed hard into other rocks. Over millions of years the action of the weather reduces mountains to sand and gravel.

Meanwhile, other processes are at work below the surface. Water, trickling down among the particles, dissolves chemical compounds from them. The dissolved compounds react with others. The rainwater turns into a complex chemical solution, producing holes in the rocks. Beneath all the pebbles, gravel, and small grains this solution attacks and erodes the upper surface of the underlying bedrock, releasing more

## SOIL EROSION

Soil particles are constantly being washed away by rain and blown away by wind. This is erosion. It is a serious problem if soil is lost by erosion faster than new soil is formed. Plant roots help hold soil particles together, and this reduces the rate of erosion. Plowing exposes the soil and is a main cause of erosion. Modern farming methods aim to keep plowing to a minimum, or eliminate it altogether, to combat erosion. Erosion is also severe where forests are cleared from steep hillsides, allowing the rain to wash the soil into the valley.

▶ Water has washed away the soil from the hillside to make this gully. This is severe soil erosion.

particles and more chemical compounds. This is chemical weathering, and it forms part of the overall weathering process.

## Arrival of Plants

Among the dissolved compounds are some that are useful to plants. Lichens are the first living organisms to take up residence. Part algae (or cyanobacteria) and part fungi, they send fine strands into tiny rock crevices to find nutrients, at the same time as making sugars by photosynthesis.

Lichens prepare the way for mosses. Mosses cling to the irregularities on the rock surface and absorb waste products left by the lichens. Then seeds from flowering plants take hold, growing in the layer of waste material left by the mosses. By this stage rock has become soil.

## How Soil Develops

The rate at which soil forms, and the type of soil that results, depends on the climate. In polar regions the ground is cold all year and frozen for much of the time. Chemical reactions go on more slowly at low temperatures, and most plants cannot grow when it is colder than about 40°F (5°C). Consequently, soil develops very

## SOIL-CLASS TRIANGLE

The soil-class triangle classifies the texture of soil according to the proportion of sand, silt, and clay particles it contains.

The proportions of at least two parts of the soil are plotted on the triangle. For example, with a soil sample containing 20 percent clay and 40 percent silt, a line is drawn parallel to the sand axis from the 20 percent point on the clay axis:

a second line is drawn parallel to the clay axis from the 40 percent point on the silt axis. Where the lines cross is the classification of the soil—in this case, loam.

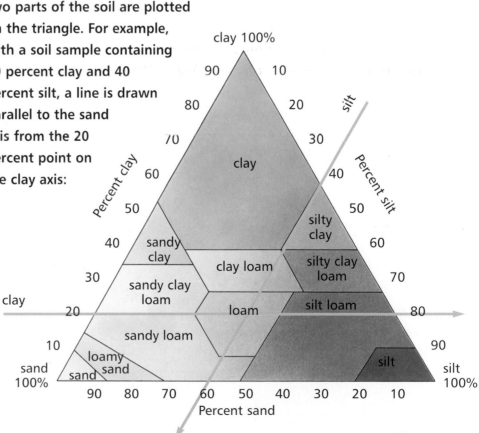

**See Also** | *FUNGI **6** 30* | *LICHENS **6** 48* | *MOSSES **7** 8* ◉

## PLANTS, CLIMATE, AND SOIL

In the tundra of northern Russia the climate is too cold for trees. Lichens and mosses are the dominant plants. The soil is thin, poorly developed, and has a perma-nently frozen layer (permafrost) below the surface. Trees are able to grow farther south in the taiga. Their roots and the smaller plants growing on the surface help build a deep, fertile soil. Still farther south the climate is too dry for trees, and the forest gives way to steppe grassland. Grassland soils are very fertile. The climate of the continental interior is too dry even for grass. It is desert, with little or no soil development.

peat
hardpan
permafrost

**Tundra:** In the snowy north the growing season is about 90 days a year. Permafrost causes poorly drained, low-nutrient soils.

topsoil

subsoil

bedrock

**Taiga:** A temperate climate means that plants can grow for half of the year. In forests minerals are quickly recycled.

nutrient layer

**Steppe:** Decreasing rainfall, and a rise in temperature, means trees give way to grass. Evaporation removes water from the soil and carries nutrients to the surface. Plants grow for most of the year while there is adequate moisture.

slowly in high latitudes. Such cold-climate soils are said to be young because their development has not gone very far.

Hot deserts are warm enough, but soil develops through the action of water, and deserts are too dry. They are also too dry for most plants. Soils develop only very slowly; and although there is plenty of sand and dust, they are just that—sand and dust, not soil.

In the tropics there is both warmth and abundant water. This is where soils develop fastest, and plants grow most exuberantly. There is such rapid growth,

however, that plants have removed almost all the mineral nutrients. They are recycled rapidly; but with each recycling some nutri-ents are lost, drained into rivers and carried away. Equatorial soils are very depleted of nutrients; they are said to be old soils.

In the middle latitudes (the temperate zones) summers are warm and winters cool, and in most places there is enough rain to sustain plants. Soils here are the most fertile in the world. Mineral nutrients are still being released from the underlying rock, and decaying plant and animal

remains create gaps in the soil, allowing air to penetrate and air-breathing organisms to thrive.

As the soil matures, it often develops distinct layers, called "horizons." Decaying plant and animal material is the top layer, and the bottom layer is the rock, called the "parent material," from which the soil is forming. The horizons are clearly visible in the vertical profile of a trench cut through the soil.

Plant roots penetrate the soil in search of water and nutrients. When the plant dies, its roots slowly decay, but the channels the roots made in the soil remain a bit longer. The tunnels made by worms, and other animals, as they search for food also remain after they have passed. The channels allow air to circulate and water to percolate. Fine particles and dissolved minerals can be washed out (leached) by rainwater.

Once the soil supports a vigorous living community, its fertility is enhanced. Cells in plant roots need air for respiration. The channels that allow water to drain also allow air to enter. This sustains animals and microorganisms in the soil that require oxygen.

▶ Where soil has been washed away from the bank, it exposes the roots of a beech tree penetrating deep into the soil.

## SOIL PROFILES

$A_0$ is the layer of litter (thin in grassland); $A_1$ is the humus-rich layer, and $A_2$ the topsoil from which particles and minerals are leached. There is much less leaching in grassland soil than forests. Horizon B is the subsoil in which leached materials accumulate. In forests $B_1$ is a transition layer, like $A_2$ at the top and $B_2$ at the bottom. $B_2$ contains particles accumulated from $A_2$ and always has more clay than $A_2$. Tree roots often reach $B_1$. The C horizon is the degraded parent rock.

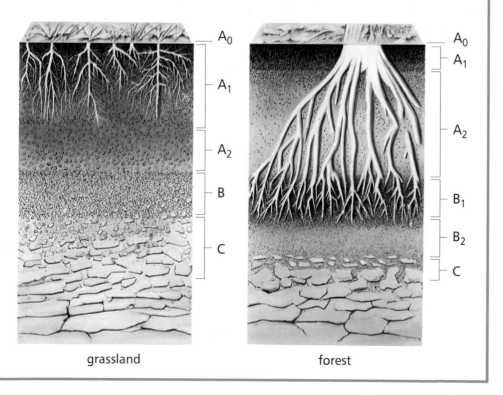

grassland

forest

**See Also** | RESPIRATION 3 10 | NUTRITION 3 30 | COLONIZATION 4 22 👁

# Colonization

WHEN LAND IS CLEARED AND LEFT BARE, either by man or nature, plants start to colonize it within days. The plants arise from seeds already in the soil, waiting for the chance to sprout, or from "imported" seeds that take the opportunity to use newly available resources. After a few weeks the site will be covered with plants.

In order to release their seeds as soon as possible, new colonies of plants reproduce quickly. Most seeds will be tiny, attached to a tuft of fine, white hairs called a pappus that catches the wind, detaching the seed from the plant and carrying it through the air.

The arrival of the first plants in a new environment is called colonization. Clouds of airborne seeds provide a clue to how it works. Each plant produces large quantities of tiny seeds that are carried by the wind, but seldom travel far. Ones that succeed in sprouting and growing into new plants will have fallen onto bare ground close to their parents. They succeed, in part, because they arrive ahead of the seeds of most other plants.

Rosebay willowherb is often one of the first to arrive. It springs up so quickly on ground that has been cleared by fire that it is also called "fireweed." It became quite common in Europe during the 20th century, probably because wars left many demolition sites. Groundsel is another early arrival.

## Getting Started

On arriving, new colonizers must sprout at once. The young seedlings will be so crowded that many of them will die. Small seeds contain little nutrient to sustain the young plant, and the surviving seedlings will also die unless light, water, and nourishment are immediately available.

It may seem wasteful to produce such vast numbers of seeds when only a few can survive, but overproduction serves a useful purpose. Each seed is slightly different from the rest and has different requirements. This means that whatever the climate and soil conditions, there is a chance that some of the seeds will find them suitable for growth. They will grow into plants that produce seeds of their own and will pass on to the next generation the characteristics that equipped them for life on that site.

## Sun-lovers

On open ground the first colonizers will be sun-loving plants. The brighter the light, the faster they will be able to make sugars by photosynthesis.

After dispersing their seeds, most colonizing plants die. Their seeds fall close to the parent plants, so a new generation of plants will appear, but by then conditions may have changed. Other plants arrive to compete for the resources. As they thrive, the early colonizers become fewer in number. Some colonizers, found among trees, will fail to flower and set seed because they are shaded. They are likely to have grown from seeds that drifted in from elsewhere. Crowded out, overshadowed, and starved of nourishment, they will eventually die out. They are not lost, but can be seen growing robustly on open ground somewhere else. This is the way early colonizers live.

## Colonizing Poisoned Ground

There are several reasons land may be bare, and one is that the soil may be contaminated. In the past wastes from mining, metal-working, and other industries have not been effectively cleared.

# Plants & Plant Life

pg. 4. - Chemical reactions that produce sugars from carbon dioxide and water. - called photosynthesis.

<u>Energy from</u> — sun + <u>sugars & minerals</u> from the ground/soil, constantly pass from one group of living organisms to another.

pg 4. <u>Carbon Cycle</u>
Burning coal, oil, and gas returns into air carbon that was stored millions of years ago, this may disturb the balance of the $CO_2$ cycle, possibly altering the climate and increase temperatures on earth.
however, ex: if plants catch onfire the carbon sent into the air is the small amount the plants used through photosynthesis.

pg 16 <u>Nitrogen Cycle</u>

air — 78% nitrogen by volume, inhale but exhale it again unaltered. Animals obtain $NO_3$ from plants they eat.

- #Some nitrogen can come from
lightning - ex: lightning releases enough
energy to force $NO_3$ to react w/ oxygen.
Oxidized nitrogen dissolves in cloud
droplets where it forms nitric acid
which then was washes to the ground
by rain. that plants can now use.
* Nitric acid changes to nitrate.

Nitrogen Fixation.
- organisms in soil react with the $NO_3$,
thes organisms make $NO_3$ react
with Hydrogen to form ammonia.
this is called (Nitrogen Fixation)
- too much of this bacteria can
infect roots of certain plants.
ex: bean family/types.

pg 17. Nitrate and ammonia are both
soluble in water and plant roots
absorb it in liquid form.

▼ Plants colonize walls either by clinging to irregularities in the stone surface, like the lichens, or by growing in the narrow crevices between the stones, like the stonecrops growing on this flint wall.

Today, naturally tolerant plants are used to remove poisons from polluted land—a process called phytoremediation. Alfalfa, Indian mustard greens, and poplar trees are some of the plants used for this purpose in the United States.

Contaminated ground may remain bare for a long time, but eventually plants will appear, although there will be fewer species. The variations that allow plants to colonize most sites also extend to toxins. If they are able to produce seed, they will pass on the genetic information necessary for survival. The first plant found to be tolerant of mine waste was bent grass, or colonial bent, a European species widely grown in American lawns and golf courses.

▲ Trees can colonize sites where enough soil accumulates between rocks. Silver birches are sun-loving trees that produce abundant seeds and are often the first trees to colonize a habitat.

▶ Coastal sand dunes are too salty for most plants. This is sea spurge, a typical coastal plant that can tolerate salty conditions.

*See Also* | GERMINATION *1* 44 | DISPERSAL OF FRUITS & SEEDS *2* 36 👁

# Succession

AS THE EARLY COLONIZERS disappear, other plants arrive to replace them. In time they, too, are replaced. Gradually, the predominant vegetation changes, and what began as open ground is transformed, perhaps into grassland or into dense scrub, then into open woodland, and finally into forest. This sequence of events, in which one group of plants displaces another, is called a succession.

Succession is a haphazard process: seeds arrive in no particular order. Colonizers sprout and grow quickly from wind-dispersed seeds. Birds deliver seeds of the fruits they eat that pass unaltered through their digestive systems and fall in their droppings. Small mammals in search of food bring seeds clinging to their fur from plants they brushed against elsewhere.

Most seeds will be from nearby plants, but some may have traveled a long way. Mammals do not usually go far, but birds sometimes fly long distances in their search for food. Seeds carried by the wind can be lifted to great heights and transported hundreds of miles before they fall to the ground. So the site receives an unpredictable assortment of seeds.

## Altering the Surroundings

Only plants that can tolerate the conditions of the site will survive; those that do will prosper. They will produce the most seed; their descendants will be widespread.

As they grow, the plants alter their surroundings in ways that favor certain plants or produce intolerable conditions for others. They remove certain minerals from the soil, absorb some of the water, making the ground drier, and shade the ground nearby.

They may also exude substances from their roots that prevent certain plants from growing near them. Poverty grass, for example, releases substances that slow the action of nitrogen-fixing bacteria. This means the soil contains enough nitrogen for the modest needs of the poverty grass, but too little for the little bluestem grass, a taller plant that would otherwise replace it.

Alder trees have nodules of nitrogen-fixing bacteria on their roots. This allows them to grow well in low-nitrogen soils. If the alders establish themselves in areas from which Douglas firs have been cleared, they grow faster than the firs and shade the fir seedlings. This can delay regeneration of the Douglas firs for years.

The preferences of plant-eating animals also affect succession. Cattle and horses do not like thorns. Consequently, by eating tree seedlings, but not thorny plants, they encourage the development of impenetrable thickets. Then young trees grow up protected by the thorns and, in time, cast so much shade that the low-growing thorny plants die.

## Reaching a Climax

Chance plays a major part in the many ways a succession proceeds. There is no reason to suppose it will follow the same sequence twice on the same site.

Ultimately, a time comes when a community is so established that its composition barely changes. As individuals die, seeds produced by plants of the same species grow to replace them. This is the "climax" type of vegetation. Once reached, this stage is likely to endure, unaltered, for many years, until a major outside disturbance, such as a change in climate, produces a new set of growing conditions.

# PLANT SUCCESSION

Plant succession can lead to a change in the vegetation in a habitat. For example, ponds can eventually become dry land. Soil particles washed from the banks and decaying plant and animal material accumulate on the bottom. This raises the bed, making the pond shallower, especially at the edges. Over time the area becomes no more than a hollow that fills with water when it rains, and land plants occupy the area.

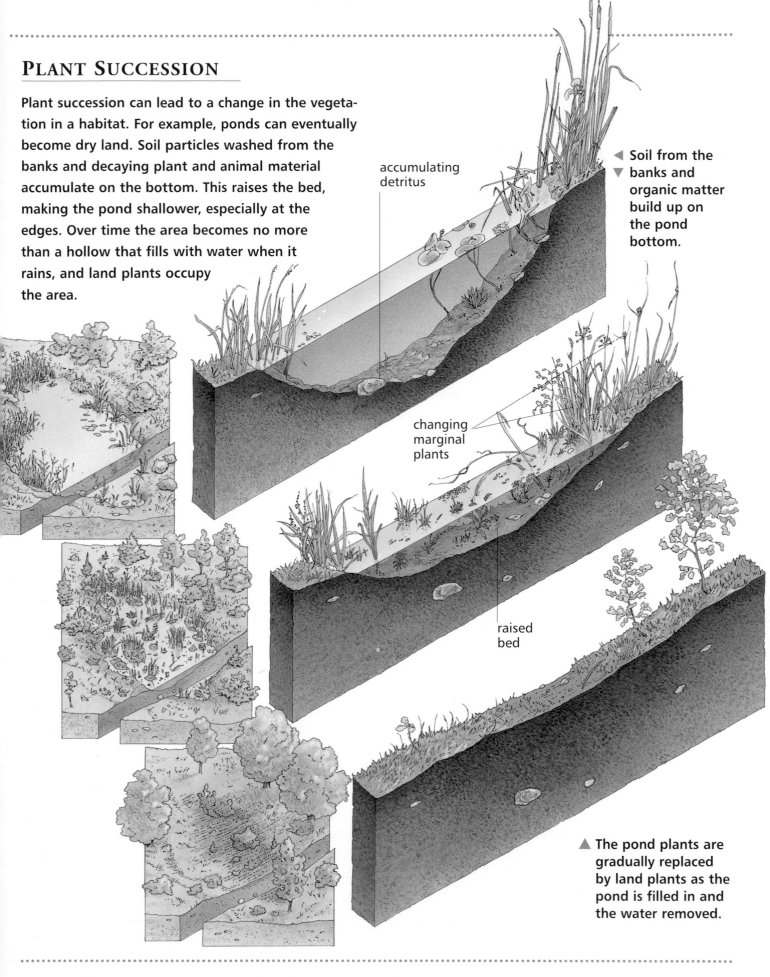

accumulating detritus

◀ Soil from the
▼ banks and organic matter build up on the pond bottom.

changing marginal plants

raised bed

▲ The pond plants are gradually replaced by land plants as the pond is filled in and the water removed.

See Also | NITROGEN FIXATION 3 34 | COLONIZATION 4 22 | DOUGLAS FIRS 8 24 ◉

# Zonation

AS YOU CLIMB A MOUNTAIN OR CROSS A BEACH TOWARD THE SEA, the type of vegetation you see growing around you changes. This is called zonation. Different communities of plants and animals live in different zones according to the climatic and chemical (biogeographical) conditions that suit them.

At sea level in the tropics you may find lush forest. As you climb, some trees will disappear as others become more common. You will eventually reach a height where there are no trees at all. This marks the tree-line—the height beyond which the climate is too cold for trees to grow. Broad-leaved trees, such as oaks and maples, will not grow unless there are at least about 120 days a year when the temperature rises above 50°F (10°C). Conif-erous trees, such as pines and firs, need only about 30 days warmer than 50°F (10°C) to survive. Consequently, coniferous trees are found where it is too cold for broad-leaved trees.

The height of the treeline depends on several factors: how shaded the area is, as well as how exposed to the wind. It also varies with latitude; nearer the equator temperatures tend to be higher. Temperature decreases with increasing height by an average 3.5°F for every 1,000 feet (6.5°C per km). In the Sierra Nevada the treeline is at about 11,500 feet (3,500 m); in the Alps of central Europe it is at 6,800 feet (2,000 m); and in New Guinea, close to the equator, it is at 12,600 feet (3,800 m).

On a graph of the temperature change against height for a moun-tainside the resulting slope is called an environmental gradient. Changes in the type of vegetation across such a gradient are called zonation.

▲ The treeline in the Italian Alps. Other plants grow higher than this, but near the summits it is too cold for any plants to survive.

## Shore Zones

Zonation is clear to see on a mountain, and it is just as clear on a rocky seashore, where the zonation is due to chemical changes, not to a change in height. The zones are bands

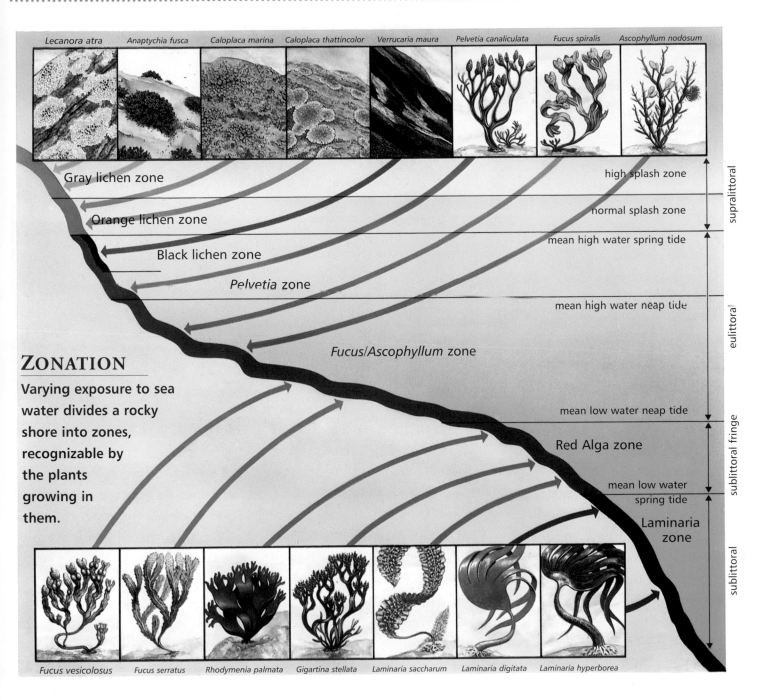

Lecanora atra    Anaptychia fusca    Caloplaca marina    Caloplaca thattincolor    Verrucaria maura    Pelvetia canaliculata    Fucus spiralis    Ascophyllum nodosum

Gray lichen zone

Orange lichen zone

Black lichen zone

*Pelvetia* zone

high splash zone

normal splash zone

mean high water spring tide

mean high water neap tide

*Fucus/Ascophyllum* zone

## ZONATION

Varying exposure to sea water divides a rocky shore into zones, recognizable by the plants growing in them.

mean low water neap tide

Red Alga zone

mean low water spring tide

Laminaria zone

supralittoral

eulittoral

sublittoral fringe

sublittoral

Fucus vesicolosus    Fucus serratus    Rhodymenia palmata    Gigartina stellata    Laminaria saccharum    Laminaria digitata    Laminaria hyperborea

parallel to the shore. They reflect the extent to which the surface is exposed to seawater, and each zone can be identified by the types of seaweed growing in it.

In the sublittoral zone, which is under water except at the lowest spring tides, there are kelp species. Above them red seaweeds grow in

the sublittoral fringe, which is uncovered at mean low spring tides. The eulittoral zone (uncovered at low neap tides) supports various species of wracks.

The next zone is one that is covered with water only at high spring tides, and the final zone is a region that is never covered with

seawater, but is sometimes splashed by it (the splash zone). Land plants, and especially lichens, are able to grow in these zones, which are identified by the color of the lichens in them. Black, orange, and gray lichens predominate with increasing distance from the sea.

***See Also*** | *RED ALGAE **6** 20* | *BROWN ALGAE **6** 26* | *WHAT IS A CONIFER? **8** 4* 👁

# Competition and Plant Defenses

PLANTS NEED LIGHT, WATER, AND MINERAL NUTRIENTS in order to thrive, but they must compete with neighboring plants for all the resources they require. As a plant grows, its leaves may shade smaller plants also competing for light, and the resources it absorbs are not available for others. Many plants also have unique survival strategies that enable them to defend themselves against predators and disease.

Some plants compete for resources by growing bigger and faster than their competitors. After their seeds have sprouted, they grow deep, extensive roots that seize water and nutrients. At the same time, they spread their leaves wide to catch the light, shading rival plants. Large plants tend to succeed at the expense of smaller ones.

Himalayan balsam is typically up to three feet (1 m) tall and grows on wet ground and riverbanks. Each spring its shoots emerge through the remains of the previous year's growth, and in a few weeks it completely covers the area with a dense mass of plants that makes it impossible for any other plant to survive.

Bracken competes in the same way. Each summer it blankets the area it occupies, spreading by means of underground stems—rhizomes—from which vertical stems and leaves emerge. The plant dies down in the fall, but its decaying leaves form a dense mat that suppresses other plants.

## Opportunist Colonizers

Farmers try to imitate this type of competition. By sowing large numbers of seeds that grow rapidly into a dense cover of vegetation, they hope that their crops will seize all the resources they need and shade out competitors.

This method is not entirely successful because there are other ways to compete, and weeds use them. When land is prepared for sowing, for a time it is left bare. This is an opportunity for colonizing plants, which grow quickly, to gain an advantage over the crop. They may be better suited than the crop for life in the field and so continue to grow with it.

If the crop consists of densely packed plants, like grass in a lawn, weeds adopt a different strategy. They spread their leaves to cover a small patch of ground, producing flowers and seeds rapidly whenever a chance occurs.

## Poisoning Rivals

Grapevines do not grow well close to radishes or laurel, and no other

▲ Cacti have sharp spines that keep animals from piercing the plant to obtain the water stored inside. There are no spines on the flowers, which need insect pollinators.

plant will grow close to a black walnut tree. The plants deter rivals with chemicals released from their roots or leaves. In some cases rain washes the poison from dead plant material lying on the ground. This keeps other species away, as well as other members of the plant's own species.

Chamise and sagebrush, two shrubs that grow in the California chaparral, use this technique to keep competitors at bay.

▲ Sagebrush, seen here in the foothills of the Rocky Mountains in Montana, poisons competitors.

Poisons produced by chamise are soluble in water; the winter rains wash them from the leaves of the plants into the soil. Grasses and other small, nonwoody plants will not grow beneath chamise, and some plants will not grow even close to it. Sagebrush releases its poisons into the air, and its bushes are often surrounded by bare ground up to 3 feet (1 m) in diameter.

## POISONING RIVALS

In the chaparral sagebrush releases terpenes, and chamise releases phenols and phenolic acids, substances that prevent other plants from growing nearby. Every 20–35 years fire destroys the vegetation. Grasses and herbs then grow rapidly, releasing seed that remains in the soil. Eventually, new chamise and sagebrush bushes grow up, and the other plants disappear.

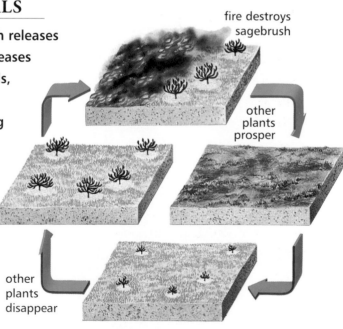

fire destroys sagebrush

other plants prosper

other plants disappear

sagebrush starts to regrow

*See Also* | *STEMS 1 28* | *SEEDS 2 28* | *SURVIVING EXTREMES 3 42* 👁

Competing plants are not to be defeated, however. Every 20 to 35 years the chaparral catches fire: all vegetation above ground is destroyed. When the ground cools, grasses and other small plants grow from dormant seeds in the soil. They flower, producing a crop of seed before the chamise and sagebrush recover and suppress them. The seeds remain in the soil until the next fire.

## Taking Advantage of Fire

Fire is common in the parts of the world where the weather includes

a dry season. The fire starts naturally, from a lightning strike or chance spark, and it can quickly destroy all the surface vegetation. The plants soon return, but for a time the ground is bare.

In the soil there are seeds lying dormant that can quickly sprout and grow on the exposed site. Quaking aspen, balsam poplar, and paper birch produce copious quantities of seed that are dispersed widely. As the ground cools, their seedlings emerge. The trees grow fast, flower, and produce a new crop of seed. By this stage other, taller trees will be starting to shade them, so they die, leaving their seeds to await the next fire.

Coast redwood and Sierra redwood trees have thick, very spongy bark. It does not burn readily, and it is thick enough to insulate the living tissue beneath. Fire seldom harms them. Other trees, such as pitch pine and longleaf pine, need fire. Their cones remain tightly closed on the tree until a fire heats them. Then the cones open, and the seeds fall into the ash. Like colonizing plants, they take advantage of bare land, but with a difference: they inhabit

▲ ◀ **The wheat crop (above) has been treated with herbicides. Corn poppy and corn marigold are flourishing on unsprayed ground (left).**

land that is naturally made bare by fire every few years.

## Protection against Plant-eaters

Plants also have mechanisms to protect themselves from being eaten by animals. They can rely on physical defenses: thorns and sharp spines, like those found on cacti, are effective deterrents. Some plants are poisonous to the touch. Poison ivy exudes a resin that causes intense skin irritation. Giant hogweed makes the skin sensitive to ultraviolet light. Stinging nettles cause an irritating, though not serious, rash.

Another method is to produce poisons. There are two types: the first makes the plant difficult or unpleasant to eat, or indigestible; the other gives the plant a smell and taste that animals find

◀ ▲ In winter (above) trees are leafless, and light reaches the ground. Herbs emerge and flower in spring before the leaf canopy closes, blocking out the light.

revolting and in some cases makes the plant toxic.

Oak trees are among the many plants that produce tannin in their leaves. Tannins inactivate digestive enzymes, so the leaves are indigestible. Animals soon learn to avoid tannin-rich leaves. Bracken also produces tannin in its mature leaves. Its young leaves contain a compound of cyanide.

Many plants release their poisons only in response to an attack, and then they release them in all their leaves, not just the one that was bitten. White clover releases hydrogen cyanide when it is attacked, and there are plants that start to convert sugars into tannins. Other plants produce hormones that interfere with the reproductive cycle of animals. For example, members of the pea and bean family (Fabaceae) produce

substances that mimic the mammalian hormone estrogen.

Most plant poisons deter plant-eaters, but some can kill. Yew, deadly nightshade, hemlock, and milkweed are among the most dangerously poisonous plants.

An animal that can survive the poison and digest the plant material has an obvious advantage, and

some have evolved ways of doing this. The most famous example is the monarch butterfly. Its caterpillars feed on milkweed, storing the poison harmlessly in their bodies. The poison remains in the bodies of the adults, making them poisonous to predators. A bird that eats a monarch butterfly will vomit violently and never eat another.

## PROTECTING OUR WORLD

## HERBICIDES

Farmers use poisons, called herbicides, to prevent weeds from competing with their crops. Without herbicides, crop yields can be lower. However, the weeds controlled by herbicides include many wild flowers that were once common but have become rare on farmland.

Today, many farmers use herbicides sparingly to minimize harm to wild plants at field edges and road verges. It is hoped that genetic modification of crops will allow farmers to reduce the amount of herbicides they need to use to control weeds.

*See Also* | *DISPERSAL OF FRUITS & SEED 2 36* | *YEWS 8 48* 👁

# Endemism

ENDEMISM IS THE NATURAL OCCURRENCE of a species in one particular area. A species that lives naturally in only one place is said to be "endemic" to that place. For example, the Sierra redwood, or big tree, and the coast redwood are found only in California, and the dawn redwood grows naturally only in southeastern China.

There are many examples of endemic species. The Scottish primrose grows only in northeastern Scotland and on the Orkney Islands, to the north of the Scottish mainland. The Canary Islands wallflower is found only on the Canary Islands, and the Mount Cook lily grows only in the Southern Alps of South Island, New Zealand.

Some endemic species are very local indeed. The island of Santa Catalina, off Los Angeles County, California (area of 74 sq. miles; 192 sq. km), has at least seven endemics, including Catalina mahogany, Catalina manzanita, and Trask's monkeyflower.

## Plants That Were Once More Widely Distributed

Some species that now grow only in one area were once distributed over a much larger area. The three redwood trees fall into this category. Coast redwoods once grew over the whole of what are now Canada and Alaska, and parts of Asia. The dawn redwood used to grow throughout Europe and much of the United States. The ginkgo tree, a native of eastern China, is another example. About 160 million years ago it grew throughout northern Eurasia, southern Greenland, and western North America. Today it has no living relatives, but appears to be identical to fossil specimens that are 200 million years old.

If a group of related species is shrinking because, one by one, its members are becoming extinct, it is not surprising that the survivors

◀ The flycatcher plant, showing the pitcher and its lid (left) and (below) the ordinary leaves, plus pitchers, made from modified leaves with a stalk to the inflorescence. It is endemic to Australia.

▲ *Alluaudia dumosa*, a member of the Didiereaceae found only in Madagascar. It has thorny branches (right) and bears flowers around the tip of a flowering shoot (left).

are confined to ever-smaller areas. The group as a whole is nearing the end of its evolutionary life, and in the natural course of events, the endemic species will also vanish. All species become extinct eventually for entirely natural reasons. Nowadays we prevent extinctions by cultivating endangered plants.

Other species are endemic to particular places for the opposite reason. Only recently evolved, they have not yet spread outside the area where they originated.

## Island Endemics

Endemic species most often occur in very isolated places where formidable barriers make it hard for species to invade. This reduces competition and allows species to survive that might be suppressed by invading colonizers. It also allows the endemic species to evolve to produce other endemics.

Oceanic islands are especially rich in endemic species. Three-quarters of the plants native to New Zealand do not occur elsewhere, and the proportion is even higher for St. Helena and Hawaii.

Growing on some mountains in Madagascar (an island off the east coast of Africa) there are between 150 and 200 species of plants that are found nowhere else. About 80 percent of the plant species on the island—including about 18 genera and

eight plant families—are endemic. One of the endemic families is the Didiereaceae, with four genera and 11 species of plants that grow in dry places. They have sharp thorns, are thick-stemmed, and contain distinctive red pigments called betalains.

The flycatcher plant also grows in a remote area. It is found only in drier parts of the swamp lands between the Donelly River, and Cheyne Beach east of Albany in southwestern Australia. It feeds on insects (but can survive without

▲ Flowers of the Cretan ebony, a plant endemic to the island of Crete, Greece.

them), catching them in a "pitcher" about 2 inches (5 cm) long containing digestive juices.

Wherever they occur, endemic plants are endangered simply because they are naturally rare. We protect a few by cultivating them to ensure their survival. The great majority of endemics can survive only if we protect the areas in which they are found.

*See Also* | PLANTS UNDER THREAT **4** *44* | GINKGO **7** *48* | REDWOODS **8** *32* 👁

# Plants and Global Climate

PLANTS GROW NATURALLY ONLY WHERE the climate suits them. Consequently, particular types of vegetation are associated with certain climates and the parts of the world where they occur. For example, tropical rain forest is found near the equator, grasslands in the interior of continents, and forests of coniferous trees across North America and Eurasia.

Coniferous forest forms a belt that stretches around the world. The boundaries of where it grows are determined by the cli-

▼ Ocean currents carry warm water away from the equator and cool water toward it.

matic conditions found between them. Climates generally relate to distance from the equator, but other factors are also involved.

Warm air rises over equatorial regions and descends again as hot, dry air. This forms hot deserts in the tropics of both hemispheres.

Inland regions are drier than coastal regions because of their distance from the ocean and have more extreme winter and summer temperatures. Although it is too dry for forests, grasslands thrive in this climate. Ocean currents also exert a strong influence. The

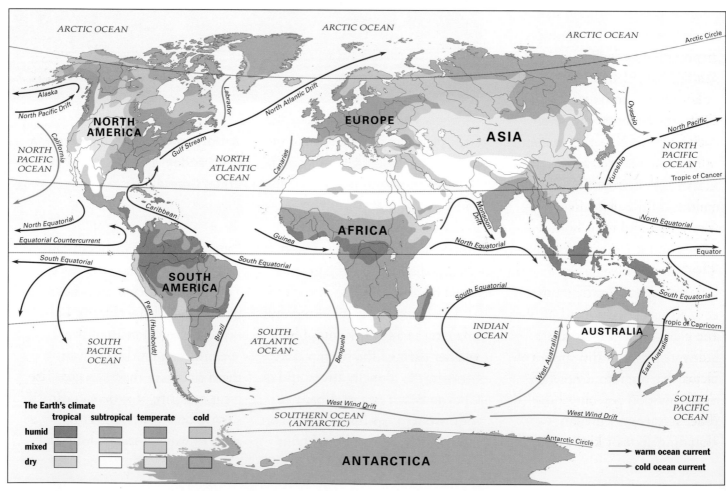

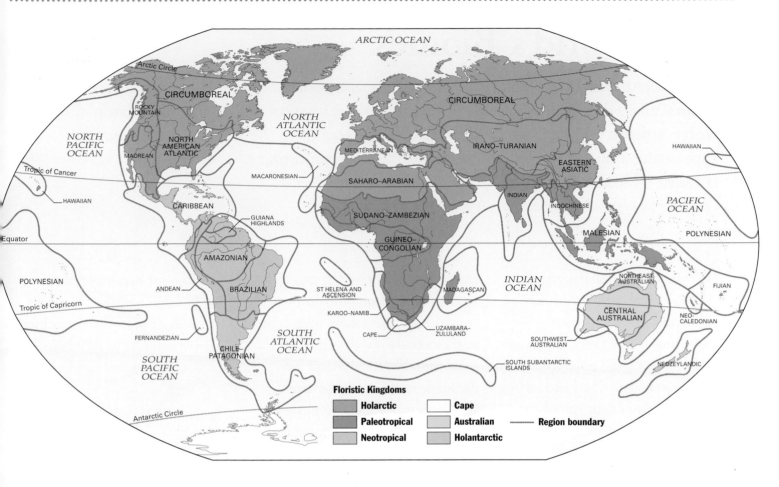

ARCTIC OCEAN

Arctic Circle
CIRCUMBOREAL
ROCKY
MOUNTAIN
CIRCUMBOREAL
NORTH
PACIFIC
OCEAN
NORTH
ATLANTIC
OCEAN
NORTH
AMERICAN
ATLANTIC
MADREAN
IRANO-TURANIAN
HAWAIIAN
MEDITERRANEAN
EASTERN
ASIATIC
Tropic of Cancer
MACARONESIAN
SAHARO-ARABIAN
INDIAN
PACIFIC
OCEAN
HAWAIIAN
CARIBBEAN
INDOCHINESE
GUIANA
HIGHLANDS
SUDANO-ZAMBEZIAN
MALESIAN
POLYNESIAN
Equator
AMAZONIAN
GUINEO-
CONGOLIAN
POLYNESIAN
ANDEAN
BRAZILIAN
ST HELENA AND
ASCENSION
MADAGASCAN
INDIAN
OCEAN
NORTHEAST
AUSTRALIAN
FIJIAN
Tropic of Capricorn
KAROO-NAMIB
CENTRAL
AUSTRALIAN
NEO-
CALEDONIAN
FERNANDEZIAN
CAPE
UZAMBARA-
ZULULAND
CHILE-
PATAGONIAN
SOUTH
ATLANTIC
OCEAN
SOUTHWEST
AUSTRALIAN
SOUTH
PACIFIC
OCEAN
SOUTH SUBANTARCTIC
ISLANDS
NEOZEYLANDIC
Antarctic Circle

Floristic Kingdoms

| | | | | |
|---|---|---|---|---|
| ▮ Holarctic | | ▯ Cape | | |
| ▮ Paleotropical | | ▯ Australian | —— Region boundary | |
| ▮ Neotropical | | ▯ Holantarctic | | |

▲ The six floristic realms and the regions into which they are divided.

British climate is affected by air that is warmed as it crosses the Atlantic and the North Atlantic Drift washing its shores. Newfoundland receives air that is affected by the cold Labrador Current, but Britain has a much milder climate, even though Newfoundland is farther south.

## Floristic Realms

The world can also be divided into a number of zones based on the plants that grow in them. This study of where in the world particular types of plants and animals are found is called biogeography. The largest zones are known as floristic realms or kingdoms. They are further divided into floristic regions, provinces (or domains), and districts.

There are six floristic realms: the Holarctic, Paleotropical, Neotropical, Cape, Australian, and Holantarctic. The Holarctic Realm includes all of North America, Greenland, Europe, North Africa (to the north of the Atlas Mountains), Asia (to the Taurus Mountains in Turkey), and the Himalayas. Most pine, fir, and cedar trees grow naturally only to the north of the southern boundary of this realm, and palm trees grow to the south of it.

Africa (except for southern Africa), Madagascar, Arabia, India, and southern Asia all lie in the Paleotropical Realm. The Neotropical Realm includes Central America, with Baja California, the southern tip of Florida, the Caribbean islands, and South America (excluding Argentina and southern Chile). Southern Africa forms the Cape Realm. Australia and New Zealand form the Australian Realm, where eucalyptus trees are endemic. The Holantarctic Realm contains southern South America and Antarctica, and some islands.

**See Also** | *SURVIVING EXTREMES* **3** 42 | *THE WORLD'S BIOMES* **4** 36 | *EVOLUTION OF PLANTS* **6** 4 ◉

# The World's Biomes

PARTICULAR CLIMATIC ZONES OF THE WORLD support compatible groups of plants and animals. Frequently, animals live with certain types of vegetation: for example, wolves inhabit the northern forests. Each large area of of the world supporting a particular type of plant and animal community is called a biome. Biomes are named after the dominant type of vegetation in the environment.

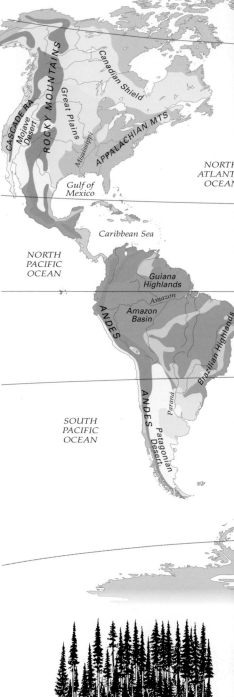

There are several distinct biomes: boreal (northern) coniferous forest and coastal coniferous forest; desert and semidesert; tundra; the polar ice caps; "Mediterranean" forest and scrub; temperate deciduous forest; tropical rain forest; seasonal tropical forest and monsoon forest; tropical grasslands and savanna; temperate grassland; mountains. Wetlands and oceans are sometimes included as biomes too.

Most of the biomes found in the Northern Hemisphere are also found in the Southern Hemisphere, although there is less land, and it does not extend so far from the equator. As a result there is little temperate forest or tundra in the Southern Hemisphere.

particular climatic zones, and each type of wetland supports its own community. The species found near coasts are not the same as those found in the wetlands on the lower reaches of large rivers, and both are different from those in bogs. So wetlands are usually included as part of the larger biome where they occur.

Oceans are often regarded as a separate biome. Many marine species live only in water at certain temperatures, so those in tropical waters are quite different from ones found in the Arctic and Antarctic. No physical barrier prevents marine animals from traveling the world, however, and many do; so the oceans are considered as one large biome.

## Wetlands and Oceans

Wetlands, such as mudflats, salt marshes, swamps, marshes, and bogs, are sometimes considered a separate biome. They support distinctive plant and animal communities, but are not confined to

## Boreal Forest and Taiga

Boreal comes from *Boreas,* the name of the Greek god of the north wind, and means northern. The band of coniferous forest that stretches around the world is called boreal forest in North

Boreal forest

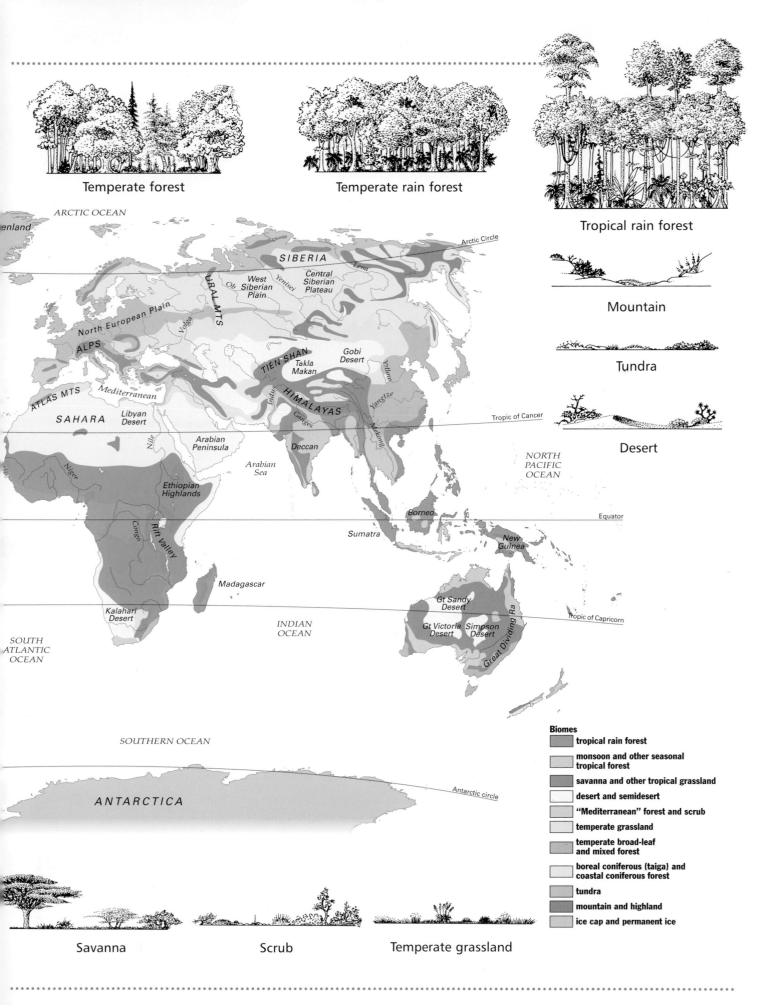

Temperate forest

Temperate rain forest

Tropical rain forest

Mountain

Tundra

Desert

ARCTIC OCEAN

Greenland

SIBERIA

Arctic Circle

URAL MTS

West Siberian Plain

Central Siberian Plateau

Ob

Yenisei

Lena

North European Plain

Volga

ALPS

TIEN SHAN

Takla Makan

Gobi Desert

Yellow

ATLAS MTS

Mediterranean

HIMALAYAS

Yangtze

Tropic of Cancer

SAHARA

Libyan Desert

Arabian Peninsula

Indus

Ganges

Deccan

Mekong

NORTH PACIFIC OCEAN

Nile

Niger

Arabian Sea

Ethiopian Highlands

Borneo

Equator

Congo

Rift Valley

Sumatra

New Guinea

Madagascar

Gt Sandy Desert

Kalahari Desert

INDIAN OCEAN

Gt Victoria Desert

Simpson Desert

Great Dividing Ra

Tropic of Capricorn

SOUTH ATLANTIC OCEAN

SOUTHERN OCEAN

Antarctic circle

ANTARCTICA

**Biomes**

- tropical rain forest
- monsoon and other seasonal tropical forest
- savanna and other tropical grassland
- desert and semidesert
- "Mediterranean" forest and scrub
- temperate grassland
- temperate broad-leaf and mixed forest
- boreal coniferous (taiga) and coastal coniferous forest
- tundra
- mountain and highland
- ice cap and permanent ice

Savanna

Scrub

Temperate grassland

**See Also** | CARNIVOROUS PLANTS **3** 36 | PLANTS AND GLOBAL CLIMATE **4** 34

America and taiga in Russia. Its composition varies with location, but predominant trees are pine, fir, larch, or spruce. In some places birch is also found.

Coastal coniferous rain forest with redwoods exists in western North America, extending southward into California.

## Tundra and Ice Caps

To the north of coniferous forest the climate is too cold and windy for trees, and in many places a layer of soil below the surface remains permanently frozen. Plant roots cannot penetrate this permafrost. As a result the plants that survive are small, with shallow roots.

The soil above the permafrost thaws in summer, but because of the frozen layer the water cannot drain away, so the ground is very wet, with pools and marshy areas that are ideal breeding grounds for mosquitoes and other insects.

This is the tundra, and it extends across North America and Eurasia. Small areas of tundra are found on islands in the Southern Hemisphere and along the coast of Antarctica.

Tundra vegetation consists of sedges, grasses, flowering herbs, mosses, and lichens, with scattered low shrubs and dwarf tree species. They include dwarf willow and arctic willow, which grow to about 6 inches (15 cm)

across, 2 inches (5 cm) tall, and dwarf birch, which reaches 6 feet (2 m) in sheltered places.

Beyond the tundra lies a region of permanent snow and ice. It supports no plants at all, although animals visit it.

## Desert and Semidesert

As you move farther from the equator, the climate becomes drier; whole years pass without rain. This produces desert with semidesert at the margins, where some rain falls in most years.

Deserts are found on all the continents. Some, such as the Gobi and Takla Makan in Asia and the central Sahara in Africa, have a dry climate since they are a long way from the ocean. Deserts at the edge of the tropics, such as the southern Sahara and the Kalahari in southern Africa, are dry because the air pressure over them is high, driving air outward. Moist air is unable to enter.

In all deserts the amount of rain that falls in the course of an average year is less than the amount that evaporates from the ground. Any rain that does fall is quickly lost, and desert plants must seize it during the brief time it is there. Cacti in America and some spurges in Africa have waxy surfaces to reduce water loss and swollen stems that store water, plus spines to protect them from animals. A few plants, such as the

creosote bush of the North American desert, survive the long drought by allowing their leaves to shrivel and die, but retain leaf buds. As rain begins, they open, and the plants start growing.

Most desert plants survive out of sight as seeds in the soil. When it rains, the seeds sprout almost instantly, and within days vegetation covers the desert surface. A few days after that the plants produce brightly colored flowers. They die after releasing their seeds, completing their life cycle before the ground dries out.

▲ Spurges (*Euphorbia* species), like those shown in the western Sahara, survive long droughts by storing water in their stems.

◀ Tundra vegetation shelters from the incessant wind by growing close to the ground. This is in Sweden.

## "Mediterranean" Forest and Chaparral

"Mediterranean" forest and scrub, such as the chaparral of North America, is found around the shores of the Mediterranean Sea, in parts of California, on the coast of Chile, in South Africa, and in parts of the southwest and south of Australia. In this biome the summers are hot and dry, the winters warm and wet.

The forest is evergreen, including some coniferous trees, such as the Aleppo pine of Europe and the Near East, and the digger pine of California, but also broad-leaved evergreen trees, such as the holm or holly oak of southern Europe and the California scrub oak. Many of the shrubs have small, leathery, water-retaining leaves. In South Africa heaths and heathers are abundant, and there are many endemic species.

## Temperate Deciduous Forest

Temperate deciduous forest originally covered most of Western Europe. It is still widespread in North America. In the Southern Hemisphere there is only a small area in the southern Andes and Tierra del Fuego.

This forest grows where rainfall is moderate, summers warm, and winters cold but short. The trees shed their leaves in winter as a way of shutting down to survive the period when water is frozen, and their roots cannot absorb it. The trees include oaks, beeches, maples, and basswoods.

In the northern part of this biome the broad-leaved trees are mixed with coniferous species. It is classified as mixed forest, where either broad-leaved or coniferous

*See Also* | WATER & WATER UPTAKE **3** 24 | SURVIVING EXTREMES **3** 42 | CACTUS FAMILY **10** 14 👁

species amount to more than 20 percent of the total.

## Tropical Rain Forest

Tropical rain forests are found to either side of the equator in South America, Africa, and southern Asia, and extend into Central America and southern India. By far the largest area of tropical rain forest is in South America.

The forests are dominated by giant trees. The treetops form a canopy of leaves about 98 feet (30 m) above the ground. Some taller trees—called emergents—protrude above the canopy and are up to 165 feet (50 m) tall. Beneath the canopy there is a level of shorter trees: many are saplings of the tall species. They will grow to their full size when a mature tree dies, creating space in the canopy. The trees are evergreen and have broad leaves, often with a pointed "drip-tip" to shed surplus water. Shrubs grow below the trees, and herbs (nonwoody plants) cover the forest floor.

Many plants live on the forest trees, using them for support. Most bromeliads found in South America are epiphytes—plants that grow on the surface of other plants. There are also climbers, some of which, such as passion flowers, bougainvilleas, and granadillas, have beautiful flowers.

Asian forests are home to another type of climber, the strangling fig. It grows from seeds dropped by birds onto a branch, which produce leaves and then roots that extend down the side of the tree to the ground. More roots appear, and they grow thicker until they completely enclose the main trunk. Then the roots merge with each other, after which the original tree usually dies, leaving a fig tree with a hollow trunk.

## Seasonal Tropical Forest and Monsoon Forest

A tropical climate, away from river valleys and other lowland areas, has pronounced wet and dry seasons. This is where seasonal tropical forest is found. The extent to which it differs from tropical rain forest depends on the amount of rainfall and the length of the dry season.

Where the dry season is short, the trees are of different—but closely related—species from those of the rain forest. The tallest emergents shed all their leaves at the onset of the dry season, but the smaller trees are evergreen. As the dry season lengthens to about five months, the forest becomes

◀ In fall temperate deciduous forest is ablaze with color as the leaves die before the harsh winter weather.

▶ Tropical rain forests have the greatest diversity of life on Earth. This is Rio Anchicaya, Colombia.

meant the tropical grasslands of Central and South America. The word is now also used to describe the grasslands covering much of Africa and northern Australia too.

Grasses are the predominant plants. During the summer rainy season, which lasts for up to seven months, they grow to more than 3 feet (1 m) tall. During the dry season they die, forming a mat of dead vegetation that often catches fire or is burned deliberately. The fire leaves a layer of ash that provides nutrients for the plants, which emerge when the rains begin. Shrubs and trees are widely scattered. Except in Australia, many of them bear thorns.

## Temperate Grasslands

Temperate grassland includes the steppe of Eurasia, veld of South Africa, prairies of North America, and pampas of South America, as well as a large area of South Island, New Zealand, where tussock grasses are common. The steppe extends from Hungary to Mongolia, and the prairies occupy much of the interior of North America from southern Alberta, Saskatchewan, and Manitoba in Canada south to Texas.

Over this vast area there are wide differences in the type of

simpler, with fewer species and areas dominated by just one or two species. In India and Burma, for example, sal and teak trees form extensive stands.

Monsoon forest grows where the wet and dry seasons are extreme—with almost no rain during the dry season, then torrential rain during the wet—and are of unequal length. In the Asian monsoon climate the dry season lasts for up to eight months. Fires are common during the dry season and affect the composition of the vegetation. The trees are widely scattered, and

their roots descend deep into the ground. Many have small leaves, which help the plants retain water through the dry season.

## Tropical Grasslands and Savanna

This open type of woodland, dominated by trees and shrubs that can withstand drought, merges into tropical grasslands and savanna. The word "savanna" comes from the Spanish *zavana* (derived from a word spoken by the inhabitants of some Caribbean islands and parts of Central America). Originally, it

grasses. There are six different types of prairie. In eastern North America the predominant grasses of the tallgrass prairie are big bluestem and Indian grass. They grow up to 10 feet (3 m) tall. Mixed prairie, which is now farmed as the wheat belt, contains a mixture of tallgrass and short-grass species. Shortgrass prairie contains buffalo grass and blue grama. Bluebunch wheatgrass grows in the bunchgrass prairie of Washington State and British Columbia, and purple needlegrass is typical of the California prairie. Desert grasslands bordering the deserts have tobosa grass and various grama and three-awn species. They grow among creosote bushes, prickly pears, other cacti, and mesquite.

## Mountains

Mountains show features of other biomes. The climate becomes more severe with increasing height; so if a mountain is close to the equator, and high enough, a journey to its summit is like one from the equator to the pole. Tropical forest at the foot of the mountain gives way to deciduous forest, then to coniferous forest, with areas of grassland. Near the top there is tundra, with permanent snow and ice above it.

The mountain biome is different in one respect, however. The plants and animals that inhabit a mountain are more closely related to species at the foot of the mountain than to those living in northern latitudes. Although the communities may be similar in

▲ The north rim of the Grand Canyon, Arizona. The sides belong to the mountain biome.

another biome, they will be composed of different species.

## American Biomes

Seven biomes occur in North America. Tundra in the far north, with a belt of coniferous forest across the continent south of it. Temperate deciduous and mixed forest occurs in southeastern Canada and the northeastern United States. "Mediterranean" forest and chaparral are in the west. Prairies (temperate grassland) lie in the center of the continent, while desert is found in the southwest. The mountain biome occurs in several areas.

*See Also* | ZONATION 4 26 | GRASS FAMILY 9 12 👁

# Plants under Threat

ALL OVER THE WORLD PLANTS ARE UNDER THREAT when land is cleared for cultivation, through competition from invading nonnative species, or when wild flowers are picked before they can set seed. Throughout history people have disturbed the natural vegetation: most of the forests of Western Europe vanished centuries ago, while in America the mixed prairie was plowed to grow wheat in the 18th century.

When people clear land, it is generally for the purpose of finding somewhere to live or growing crops. Although the natural vegetation is removed, it is not necessarily lost. It may survive elsewhere at the edges or on land that has not been cleared.

Years or even centuries later the land may no longer be needed for farming, or it may not be able to be cultivated any more due to depletion of nutrients. Then it is often abandoned. This happened over quite a large area of New England. Left to itself, within a very short time a plant succession leads to a community little different from the one that was cleared initially. It is still possible to make out many of the old field boundaries in what are now the forests of New England. Change need not mean permanent loss.

## Recolonization

For a habitat to recover, the original species of plants must be able to colonize the area. The New England forests recovered because the original species were still growing near the abandoned land. Their seeds accumulated on the land, and many smaller plants, still present as seeds in the soil, were waiting to sprout.

Even in the most intensively farmed areas, where weeds have

been kept out of the vast fields for many years, recolonization by original species has happened. Farmers in the American corn-belt found species returning soon after they reduced the amount of herbicide they sprayed each year.

## Risk to Tropical Forest

Tropical forest, too, usually grows back again if the cleared land is left alone, provided it is left alone for the 80–100 years it takes for the forest to regenerate. This occurs in areas that have been cleared by logging. Once the trees have been felled, the land is abandoned by the loggers; there is no point in returning until it has fully regenerated. Provided farmers do not move in, the original vegetation eventually returns.

When tropical rain forest is cleared permanently, however, some plant species may become extinct. This is because many smaller plants of the tropical rain forest occur in few places. They have evolved over the millions of years that parts of the rain forest have existed, so they are endemic to certain areas. Rain forest is so rich in species, and covers such a vast area, that scientists have not been able to catalog all the plants it holds. There is no way of knowing if species are lost, or how many, when forest is cleared.

## Ranching and Farming

The most serious threats to plant survival are ranching and traditional farming. Large areas of forest have been converted to cattle ranches. Cattle trample or eat tree seedlings as soon as they emerge, preventing the original vegetation from returning.

▲ *Cyclamen mirabile*, native to Anatolia, Turkey, was threatened by collection. It is now grown in nurseries for sale to gardeners.

◄ A hillside farm in East Africa. The cattle prevent the forest from returning.

45

◀ **Slash-and-burn farming in the Brazilian tropical rain forest. Crops are grown on the cleared land.**

Traditional "slash-and-burn" farming involves clearing a small area of forest by felling the trees, removing any plant material needed for building or other purposes, then burning what remains. Seeds are sown in the ashes, and crops are grown on the site for about three years, by which time tree seedlings and other wild plants crowd out the cultivated plants, and crop yields fall. The site is then abandoned, and the slash-and-burn operation repeated on another site nearby. Each family has several plots of land, and they visit each in turn.

At one time the farmers would have left each site long enough for the forest to regrow, so there was no permanent damage to the forest. But a farming family needs a large area to produce enough food for its members. In some places there are too many people living and working on the land, so farmers are forced to return to sites before they have regenerated. This means some plants may not have completed their life cycle, and in time the soil will not contain any of their seeds, and the plants will be lost forever.

The United Nations Food and Agriculture Organization

## PROTECTING OUR WORLD

## SLASH AND BURN: GOOD AND BAD

Slash-and-burn farming, also called "shifting cultivation," was practiced in Europe centuries ago, but trees were not given sufficient time to grow back on the cultivated plots. This led eventually to the clearance of most of the original temperate forest. In the tropics, where higher temperatures mean growth is much faster, it takes less time for the forest to return. Slash-and-burn farming is sustainable provided it is based on small plots and allows a long period between the cultivation of each of them.

However, crop yields are often low, and attempts to increase output lead to plots being tilled before the forest has returned. This reduces soil fertility, so ultimately the forest trees are unable to return. More efficient alternatives to slash-and-burn farming are badly needed.

▲ **Common lantana growing in Hawaii, where it is a weed that suppresses native plants.**

estimates that the total area of tropical forests is decreasing each year by about 0.7 percent in Africa, 1.1 percent in Asia, 0.1 percent in Oceania (islands of the tropical Pacific), 1.3 percent in North and Central America, and 0.6 percent in South America. The percentages sound small, but Brazil may be losing its forest at the rate of almost 3 million acres (1.2 million hectares) a year.

## Collecting Wild Plants

Collecting plants can also drive them to extinction. Gathering wild flowers for decoration is harmless if only a few of the flowers are picked. However, if all of them are taken, and they are picked just as the flower buds are opening, no seed will be produced. After a few years the flowering plants will have vanished.

Overpicking wild flowers threatens their survival, but there is another threat. Wild plants are dug up and sold to be grown in gardens. This is a problem for plants that grow from bulbs or corms, such as cyclamens and tulips. Collected in the countries where they grow naturally and sold in other parts of the world, many species may become extinct in the wild.

## Plant Invaders

Plants are also threatened by the invasion of nonnative species. The water hyacinth, a native of tropical South American rivers, was taken to North America in 1884 by Japanese visitors attending the Cotton States Exposition in New Orleans, who liked its attractive blue flowers. It escaped into nearby rivers and lakes, where it spread rapidly, choking waterways and suppressing all the native aquatic plants. Water hyacinth was also introduced into Africa and Asia, and throughout the tropics it has become the most serious aquatic weed. It has commercial uses—it can purify water—but it is a serious danger to other plants. It reproduces from buds that break off and grow into new plants. A single water hyacinth plant can produce 30 offspring in 23 days, 1,200 in just four months.

Hawaii has been greatly affected by the introduction of nonnatives. Common lantana, a shrub belonging to the verbena family (Verbenaceae) is native to tropical America. Sold by florists and grown as a popular ornamental in the southern United States, in Hawaii it is a troublesome weed that covers large areas, choking native plants. It is also a damaging weed in parts of Asia, where it has also been introduced.

Japanese knotweed, another attractive ornamental plant, has escaped from cultivation in Britain. It is also a vigorous and troublesome weed.

## Conservation

The International Union for Conservation, Nature, and Natural Resources (IUCN), based

***See Also*** | *ENDEMISM 4 32* | *PLANTS IN HORTICULTURE 5 48* | *LILY FAMILY 9 20* ◉

in Switzerland, is drawing up lists of plants that are in danger of extinction. So far a list for Europe has been completed. Lists for other continents are to follow. Each list is a "best guess" because, although scientists have studied European and North American species, plants in other parts of the world are not as well known.

An imperfect list is better than no list at all. When a plant on the list is found, steps can be taken to ensure that it is not lost.

Efforts are also being made to eradicate the practice of digging up rare plants to sell for cultivation. Many have been added to the list of species covered by the CITES (Convention on International Trade in Endangered Species). This international agreement, reached in Washington in 1973, makes it a criminal offense to buy, sell, or be in possession of any part of one of the listed species. Enforcing the law is hard, but most governments try to do so. Responsible plant suppliers now mark packets containing bulbs to show they are from plants grown in nurseries and have not been collected in the wild. They urge their customers to check packs before they buy.

## Seed Banks

Plants can also be saved by storing them in "seed banks." The seeds of many species will sprout, even

◀ Planting trees, here in the Sierra Nevada mountains, California, prevents soil erosion.

▶ View inside the tropical biome of the Eden Project in England. Two giant "greenhouses" house a mass of plants from tropical forests and Mediterranean forest and scrub.

after being stored for 20 years, if they are first dried so that their total moisture content is about 4 percent and are kept at a constant temperature of 32°F (0°C). Most seeds take up little space, so seed banks are convenient. Every few years, samples are grown to produce a new crop of seeds that are returned to storage.

Not all plants have seeds that can be stored in this way. An alternative is to keep plant tissue taken from stems, leaves, or roots. This method preserves the genetic material, and plants can be grown from their own tissues.

## Protecting Habitats

The best way to protect plants is to prevent the destruction of their habitat, and the most effective way to do that is to reduce the demand for farmland. In the tropics, for example, "alley

cropping" is proving successful. Trees are grown in rows with farm crops in the spaces—the alleys—between the rows. The crops are sheltered but not shaded, by the trees. Mature trees are felled and replaced. This is a much more productive way of growing food than slash-and-burn farming.

Forest plantations can produce timber as a sustainable crop. They usually contain fast-growing species, such as eucalyptus, which are not the trees of the natural forest, but yield high-quality timber. The plantations occupy land that was once forest, but they make it possible to leave a much larger area of forest undisturbed.

Many people and organizations recognize that a large number of plants have become rare, while many face extinction. Improved land management, direct protection in reserves, and strict enforcement of international laws can make a big difference. Not every plant can be saved from extinction, but many can.

# Glossary

**alley cropping** A farming method in which TREES are grown in rows with farm crops in the spaces in between.

**amino acid** One of the building blocks from which proteins are constructed. All amino acids contain a carboxyl group (COOH) linked to an amino group (NH$_2$). They are linked to another group that varies with each amino acid.

**ammonia** NH$_3$, a very soluble compound that is produced by NITROGEN-FIXING BACTERIA and then converted to NITRATE.

**ammonium** NH$_4$, which forms when AMMONIA reacts with hydrogen.

**aquifer** Porous rock, gravel, soil, or other material that lies above an impermeable layer and through which GROUND WATER moves.

**bacterium** (*pl.* **bacteria**) Microscopic organism that lacks a true cell nucleus. Most are single-celled.

**bedrock** The rock that lies beneath the soil.

**bicarbonate** A hydrogen carbonate, especially carbonic acid (H$_2$CO$_3$), which forms when carbon dioxide (CO$_2$) dissolves in water (H$_2$O).

**biomass** The total mass of all the living organisms of a particular kind present in an ECOSYSTEM or at a particular level in a FOOD CHAIN.

**biome** The type of vegetation that is found over a large area. Tropical rain forests, temperate grasslands, and deserts are biomes.

**blue-green algae** *See* CYANO-BACTERIA.

**bromeliad** A plant belonging to the family Bromeliaceae; includes the pineapple and Spanish moss.

**calcium carbonate** CaCO$_3$, an insoluble salt from which seashells form.

**canopy** The foliage of forest trees.

**carbonate** A salt of carbonic acid (*See also* BICARBONATE).

**carnivore** An organism that feeds exclusively on animal flesh.

**chalk** A rock made principally from CALCIUM CARBONATE derived from seashells that accumulated on the seabed and were then compressed.

**chaparral** The scrub and forest vegetation of parts of western California and adjacent regions, consisting of TREES and SHRUBS adjusted to survive the hot, dry season.

**climax** The final stage in a vegetation SUCCESSION, at which the vegetation is in balance with its physical and chemical environment.

**cloud forest** Tropical forest on mountainsides, usually shrouded in cloud.

**colonization** The successful establishment of a newly arrived species in a HABITAT.

**community** A group of POPULATIONS of different organisms, all of which inhabit the same area.

**competitive exclusion** The ecological principle that two species, using the same resources in the same way, cannot both inhabit the same area at the same time, because one will utilize the resources more efficiently and eliminate its rival.

**condensation** The change from gas to liquid.

**conifer** A TREE that bears its seeds in cones. Conifers are classed in the phylum Coniferophyta, which includes pines, firs, spruces, and junipers.

**consumer** An organism that is unable to make complex substances from simple chemical ingredients, so must obtain food by consuming other organisms.

**cyanide** A salt of hydrocyanic acid, also called hydrogen cyanide (HCN). All cyanides are extremely poisonous. They combine with one of the enzymes involved in cell RESPIRATION and block the production of energy in cells.

**Cyanobacteria** A large and varied group (phylum) of BACTERIA that contain chlorophyll and are able to carry out PHOTOSYNTHESIS. They were formerly known as blue-green algae.

**decomposer** An organism that feeds on dead plant or animal material and breaks down the large, complex molecules from which the material is made into much smaller, simpler substances. Many BACTERIA and fungi are decomposers.

**detritus** Fragments of dead leaves, twigs, animal droppings, and dead animals that form a layer above the soil. Detritus provides a HABITAT for many organisms.

**drip tip** A point at the tip of a leaf that allows water to drain from the surface.

**ecology** The study of the relationships among organisms and between organisms and every aspect of their physical and chemical environments.

**ecosystem** All of the living organisms that inhabit an area that is distinct from adjacent areas, together with the physical and chemical features of their environment.

**emergent** A TREE that protrudes above the forest CANOPY.

**endemism** (*adj.* **endemic**) The occurrence of a species, or group of plants or animals, in a particular geographic area and nowhere else.

**epiphyte** A plant that grows on the surface of another plant, but does not take nutrients from it.

**eulittoral zone** The part of a seashore that is exposed at neap low tides.

**evaporation** The change from liquid to gas.

**floristic realm** A world region that contains a distinct type of vegetation, including ENDEMIC species or genera.

**food chain** The movement of energy, in the form of food, from organism to organism, each organism being at a different feeding level. For example, grass is eaten by cottontails, which are eaten by coyotes. This food chain can be written as:

grass → cottontail → coyote.

**food web** A diagram that represents the feeding relationships of the organisms within an ECOSYSTEM. Typically, arrows link the organisms that are eaten to the animals that eat them.

**fossil fuel** Any fuel made from the partially decomposed, and very much altered, remains of plants and animals that lived millions of years ago. It is obtained today by mining below the ground. Coal, oil, and natural gas are fossil fuels. Peat is sometimes described as a fossil fuel, although it formed more recently.

**fresh water** Water that contains no more than 0.03 percent of chlorine by weight.

**fungus** (*pl.* **fungi**) A eukaryotic organism that lacks chlorophyll and so does not PHOTOSYNTHESIZE. Fungi produce spores and do not have undulipodia (whiplike structures that propel eukaryotic organisms through water) at any stage of the life cycle.

**gas exchange** The movement of gases into and out of plants through the leaf STOMATA.

**glacier** A large mass of ice that rests on land and that moves very slowly.

**ground water** Water that accumulates below ground, above a layer of impermeable material such as clay or rock, and saturates the soil by filling all the spaces between soil particles.

**habitat** The area in which an organism or COMMUNITY lives, defined by its physical, chemical, and biological features.

**hardpan** A soil HORIZON that is hardened either chemically or as a result of being compacted by heavy machinery.

**herb** A plant with no woody parts above ground.

**herbivore** An organism that feeds exclusively on plants. In food chains they are the PRIMARY CONSUMERS.

**horizon** A distinct layer that is visible in a section cut vertically through the soil.

**ice sheet** A large mass of ice, usually more than 20,000 square miles (52,000 km2) in area.

**jetstream** A high-level wind that blows from west to east in both hemispheres.

**leaching** The removal from soil of substances that have dissolved in rain-

water and are transported by it as the water drains away. The solution removed this way is called a leachate.

**limestone** A rock largely made from CALCIUM CARBONATE derived from seashells that accumulated on the seabed and were then compressed and mixed with other ingredients.

**microhabitat** The precise location within an ECOSYSTEM where a particular organism is most likely to be found. For example, elm bark beetles live beneath the bark of elm trees, so the region beneath the elm bark is the microhabitat for those beetles.

**monsoon forest** The type of forest that occurs where there is an extreme difference between the wet and dry seasons.

**niche** The function an organism performs within an ECOSYSTEM. A niche includes the microhabitat of the organism, the organism itself, the periods of time it is found there and is active, and the resources it obtains.

**nitrate** $NO_3$, which is a salt or ester of nitric acid ($HNO_3$) and the form in which plants absorb most of the nitrogen they need.

**nitrification** The sequence of chemical reactions by which certain BACTERIA convert AMMONIA ($NH_3$) into NITRATE ($NO_3$).

**nitrite** $NO_2$, which is a salt or ester of nitrous acid ($HNO_2$).

**nitrogen fixation** (*adj.* **nitrogen-fixing**) The incorporation of molecules of nitrogen gas into compounds that can be absorbed by plants.

**nodule** A small, approximately spherical mass that is attached to the outside of the roots of certain plants, especially (but not exclusively) legumes. It contains a colony of NITROGEN-FIXING BACTERIA.

**paddy** A field that is flooded to a depth of a few inches in order to grow rice, which is planted as seedlings in the mud. The field is later drained so that the ground is dry for harvesting.

**pampas** The temperate grassland of South America.

**parent material** The rock from which a soil is derived.

**peat** Partially decomposed plant remains.

**permafrost** A layer of ground that is permanently frozen. To become permafrost, the ground must remain frozen for at least two consecutive winters and the summer between.

**photosynthesis** The process by which green plants manufacture sugar from carbon dioxide and water, using sunlight energy.

**plantation** A group of TREES, usually of the same species, that are being grown as a commercial crop.

**population** All the individuals of a particular species that inhabit a particular area.

**prairie** The temperate grassland of North America.

**primary consumer** A HERBIVORE that is a CONSUMER that feeds on PRODUCERS.

**producer** An organism that manufactures complex substances from simple chemical ingredients. Green plants are producers because they perform PHOTOSYNTHESIS.

**profile** A vertical section that is cut through soil to reveal its HORIZONS.

**protein** A complex substance made from AMINO ACIDS joined together. Enzymes, antibodies, muscle, and other tissues are made from proteins.

**respiration** The process through which cells obtain energy. Food (in the form of sugar) is broken down by a sequence of chemical reactions into progressively simpler substances; finally, carbon and hydrogen are oxidized using oxygen absorbed from the air. Carbon dioxide and water vapor are released as waste products.

**salt water** Water that contains about 3.5 percent chlorine by weight.

**savanna** The tropical grassland found in Africa.

**secondary consumer** A CARNIVORE that is a CONSUMER that feeds on PRIMARY CONSUMERS.

**seed bank** A store of plant seeds that are kept as a means of preventing the extinction of plant species.

**shrub** A woody plant that is less than 33 feet (10 m) tall and that divides near ground level into several main stems, but has no single trunk. It lives for several years and does not die back at the end of each growing season.

**slash-and-burn** A subsistence farming method. An area of forest is cleared, the vegetation burned, and crops sown in the ashes. After a few years the natural vegetation returns, and crop yields fall. The site is abandoned, and the process repeated elsewhere.

**species** A group of organisms that can breed among themselves but not with other organisms.

**splash zone** The part of a seashore that is never covered by the sea but is sometimes splashed by seawater.

**steppe** The temperate grasslands of eastern Europe and Asia.

**stomata** (*sing.* **stoma**) Pores in the surface of leaves (and stems) through which GAS EXCHANGE takes place. Carbon dioxide for PHOTOSYNTHESIS and oxygen for RESPIRATION enter the plant, and water vapor,

carbon dioxide, and oxygen leave it.

**sublittoral fringe** The part of a seashore exposed at mean low spring tides.

**sublittoral zone** The part of a seashore that is under water except at the lowest spring tides.

**subsoil** The lower soil HORIZON into which substances derived from the decomposition of material in the topsoil are washed and where they accumulate.

**succession** The sequence of plants that establish themselves in a HABITAT over a period of time. One type of vegetation follows another until a stable CLIMAX develops.

**tannin** One of a group of substances produced by plants and used to treat animal skins and hides, converting them to leather. Tannins also inactivate digestive enzymes, so plant tissues containing tannins are indigestible.

**tertiary consumer** A CARNIVORE that feeds on other carnivores and HERBIVORES.

**topsoil** The upper soil HORIZON, in which plant and animal material decomposes.

**transpiration** The loss of water from a plant by EVAPORATION, mainly through its STOMATA.

**tree** A woody plant that is more than 33 feet (10 m) tall and usually has one main trunk (although some trees have several). It lives for several years and does not die back at the end of each growing season.

**treeline** The limit beyond which the climate is too cold for TREES to grow.

**tundra** The vegetation that is found in latitudes beyond the TREELINE. It consists of grasses, sedges, mosses, lichens, and low SHRUBS.

**turgor** (*adj.* **turgid**) Rigidity due to water pressure. In plants turgor results from the pressure of water on cell walls.

**veld** The temperate grassland of southern Africa.

**waterlogged** Saturated, so that all the small spaces between soil particles have been filled by water, expelling all the air.

**water table** The upper margin of the GROUND WATER. Soil below the water table is saturated; soil above it is unsaturated.

**weathering** The physical and chemical processes by which solid rock is broken down to small grains.

# Scientific Names

*In this set common names have been used wherever possible. Listed below are the plants and animals mentioned in this volume for which scientific names have not already been given. See Volume 1, page 7 for further detail on the naming of plants.*

alders *Alnus* species
alfalfa *Medicago sativa*
Aleppo pine *Pinus halepensis*
American beech *Fagus grandifolia*
amphipods: order Amphipoda
arctic willow *Salix arctica*
aspens *Populus* species
balsam poplar *Populus balsamifera*
barn owl *Tyto alba*
basswoods *Tilia* species
beeches *Fagus* species
big bluestem *Andropogon gerardi*
birches *Betula* species
bitterling *Rhodeus amarus*
black walnut *Juglans nigra*
bladder wrack *Fucus vesiculosus*
blue grama *Bouteloua gracilis*
bluebell *Hyacinthoides non-scripta*
bluebunch wheatgrass *Elytrigia spicata*
bougainvilleas *Bougainvillea* species
bracken *Pteridium aquilinum*
bromeliads: family Bromeliaceae
buffalo grass *Buchloe dactyloides*
cacti: family Cactaceae
caddisflies: order Trichoptera
California scrub oak *Quercus dumosa*
Canary Islands wallflower *Cheiranthus scoparius*
carp *Carassius* species
cedars *Cedrus* species
chamise *Adenostoma fasciculatum*
channeled wrack *Pelvetia canaliculata*
coast redwood *Sequoia sempervirens*
common lantana *Lantana camara*
corn marigold *Chrysanthemum segetum*
corn poppy *Papaver rhoeas*
creosote bush *Larrea divaricata*
Cretan ebony *Ebenus creticus*
cyclamens *Cyclamen* species
dawn redwood *Metasequoia glyptostroboides*
deadly nightshade *Atropa belladonna*
digger pine *Pinus sabiniana*
Douglas firs *Pseudotsuga* species
dragonflies: suborder Anisoptera
dwarf birch *Betula nana*
dwarf willow *Salix herbacea*
eel *Anguilla anguilla*
eucalyptuses *Eucalyptus* species

European beech *Fagus sylvatica*
European bison *Bison bonasus*
fallow deer *Dama dama*
figs *Ficus* species
fireweed *Epilobium angustifolium*
firs *Abies* species
flycatcher plant *Cephalotus follicularis*
frogs *Rana* species
giant hogweed *Heracleum mantegazzianum*
ginkgo *Ginkgo biloba*
grama *Bouteloua* species
granadillas *Passiflora* species
grapevine *Vitis vinifera*
grasses: family Poaceae
gray squirrel *Sciurus carolinensis*
groundsel *Senecio vulgaris*
heaths, heathers *Erica* species
hedgehog *Erinaceus europaeus*
hemlock *Conium maculatum*
heron *Ardea cinerea*
Himalayan balsam *Impatiens glandulifera*
holm oak *Quercus ilex*
Indian grass *Sorghastrum nutans*
isopods: order Isopoda
jack pine *Pinus banksiana*
Japanese knotweed *Reynoutria japonica*
kelp *Laminaria* species
kingfisher *Alcedo atthis*
knotted wrack *Ascophyllum nodosum*
larch *Larix* species
laurel, bay laurel *Laurus nobilis*
limes *Tilia* species
lindens *Tilia* species
little bluestem grass *Schizachyrium scoparium*
longleaf pine *Pinus palustris*
lupins *Lupinus* species
maidenhair tree *Gingko biloba*
maples *Acer* species
mayfly larvae *Ephemera* species
mesquite *Prosopis juliflora*
milkweeds *Asclepias* species
monarch butterfly *Danaus plexippus*
mosquitoes: family Culicidae
Mount Cook lily *Ranunculus lyalli*
mute swan *Cygnus olor*
oaks *Quercus* species
palms: family Arecaceae

paper birch *Betula papyrifera*
passionflowers *Passiflora* species
pea *Pisum sativum*
pike *Esox lucius*
pines *Pinus* species
poison ivy *Rhus radicans*
poverty grass *Aristida oligantha*
prickly pears *Opuntia* species
purple needlegrass *Stipa pulchra*
quaking aspen *Populus tremuloides*
rabbit *Oryctolagus cuniculus*
radish *Raphanus sativus*
redwoods *Sequoia sempervirens*, *Sequoidendron giganteum* (big tree)
rice *Oryza sativa*
rosebay willowherb *Epilobium angustifolium*
sagebrush *Artemisia tridentata*
sal *Shorea robusta*
Scottish primrose *Primula scotica*
sea spurge *Euphorbia paralias*
sedges: family Cyperaceae
serrated wrack *Fucus serratus*
Sierra redwood (also called wellingtonia, giant sequoia, or big tree) *Sequoiadendron giganteum*
silver birch *Betula pendula*
spiral wrack *Fucus spiralis*
spruces *Picea* species
spurges: family Euphorbiaceae
stinging nettle *Urtica dioica*
stonecrops *Sedum* species
strangling figs *Ficus* species
teak *Tectona grandis*
Teesdale violet *Viola rupestris*
three-awn grasses *Aristida* species
three-spined stickleback *Gasterosteus aculeatus*
tobosa grass *Hilaria mutica*
tulips *Tulipa* species
water beetles: family Dytiscidae
water hyacinth *Eichhornia crassipes*
water snail *Viviparus viviparus*
water vole *Arvicola terrestris*
wheat *Triticum* species
white clover *Trifolium repens*
wisent *Bison bonasus*
worm *Lumbriculus variegatus*
yew *Taxus baccata*

# Set Index

# Further Reading   Volume 4: Plant Ecology

*Basics of Environmental Science* by Michael Allaby. Routledge, 2000.

*Biomes of the World* by Michael Allaby. Grolier Educational, 1999.

*Ecology* by S. Charles Kendeigh. Prentice–Hall, 1974.

*Ecosystem: Deserts* by Michael Allaby. Facts on File, 2000.

*Ecosystem: Temperate Forests* by Michael Allaby. Facts on File, 1999.

*Natural Woodland: Ecology and Conservation in Northern Temperate Regions* by George F. Peterken. Cambridge University Press, 1996.

*The Natural History of the USSR* by Algirdas Knystautas. Century Hutchinson, 1987.

*The Oxford Dictionary of Ecology* edited by Michael Allaby. Oxford University Press, 1998.

*The Plant Book* by D. J. Mabberley. Cambridge University Press, 1987.

*The Science of Ecology* by Richard Brewer. Saunders College Publishing, 1988.

---

## Useful website addresses

**Catalina's Endemic Plants**
www.catalinaconservancy.org/plants/pl_endem.htm

**The Garden of Eden in Mid-Cornwall**
ourworld.compuserve.com/homepages/mevatele/eden.htm

**Madagascar: Biodiversity that Must be Saved**
www.duke.edu/web/primate/madbiod.html

**A Marine Food Web**
www3.umassd.edu/Public/Exhibit/DES300/game/eatandbe.htm

**Monocots: Life History and Ecology**
www.ucmp.berkeley.edu/monocots/monocotlh.html

**Phytoremediation: Plants that Consume Hazardous Waste**
www.ecological–engineering.com/phytorem.html

**Plants and Our Environment**
tqjunior.advanced.org/3715/Environ.html

**Royal Botanic Gardens, Kew**
www.rbgkew.org/uk

**Texas Endemics:** Checklist of All Endemics
www.csdl.tamu.edu/FLORA/cgi/endemics_taxa_page2

**Wildlife Conservation Society**
www.wcs.org/

# Picture Credits   Volume 4: Plant Ecology

**Abbreviations**
HS Holt Studios

All photographs are Andromeda Oxford Limited copyright except:

5 HS/Inga Spence; 13 HS; 15 HS/Inga Spence; 17 HS/Nigel Cattlin; 19 HS/Inga Spence; 21 HS/Primrose Peacock; 23tl Chris Munday; 23tr Martin Anderson; 23b G. Bateman; 26 HS/Gordon Roberts; 29 and 30c HS/Nigel Cattlin; 30b HS/Duncan Smith; 30–31 and 31 G. Bateman; 33 HS/Bob Gibbons; 38–39 HS/January; 39 HS/Hew Prendergast; 40 HS; 41 HS/Nigel Cattlin; 42 HS/Dick Roberts; 43 HS/Willem Harinck; 44–45 Planet Earth Pictures/Sean Avery; 45 Harry Smith Horticultural Photographic Collection; 46 HS/Irene Lengui; 47 Frans Lanting/Bruce Coleman Collection; 48 HS/Inga Spence; 49 Martin Anderson

*While every effort has been made to trace the copyright holders of illustrations reproduced in this book, the publishers will be pleased to rectify any omissions or inaccuracies.*